UNTOLD LIVES:
THE FIRST GENERATION OF
AMERICAN WOMEN PSYCHOLOGISTS

UNTOLD LIVES: THE FIRST GENERATION OF AMERICAN WOMEN PSYCHOLOGISTS

Elizabeth Scarborough and
Laurel Furumoto

Columbia University Press   New York   1987

Library of Congress Cataloging-in-Publication Data

Scarborough, Elizabeth.
  Untold lives.

  Bibliography: p.
  Includes index.
  1. Women psychologists—United States—Biography.
2. Psychology—United States—History—19th century.
3. Psychology—United States—History. I. Furumoto,
Laurel. II. Title.
BF109.A1S24 1987   150'.88042   86-20715
ISBN 0-231-05154-9

Columbia University Press
New York   Guildford, Surrey
Copyright © 1987 Columbia University Press
All rights reserved

Printed in the United States of America

Book design by Ken Venezio

*To the memory of Edna Heidbreder (1890–1985),
beloved friend and distinguished psychologist of
an earlier generation, and to future generations
of women psychologists*

Contents

Illustrations

Preface and Acknowledgments

The initial impetus for this book came when we were invited to participate in a symposium organized by Thomas C. Cadwallader of Indiana State University for the 1974 meeting of the Eastern Psychological Association. He wanted to feature the careers of psychology's first three eminent women: Christine Ladd-Franklin, Mary Whiton Calkins, and Margaret Floy Washburn. He and his wife Joyce Cadwallader had worked with the Ladd-Franklin papers. He knew that Laurel Furumoto, a member of the psychology faculty at Wellesley College, was interested in history and would have access to materials on Calkins. No one had shown interest in Washburn, so Cadwallader recruited Elizabeth Scarborough Goodman, a recent Ph.D. in history of psychology who was then unemployed, to put together a paper on her.

Thus began our involvement with early women psychologists and the conditions that influenced their careers. We were fascinated with them as individuals and as our foremothers in psychology and were surprised that so little had been written about these outstanding women. Gradually we became aware of the difficulties of retrieving information about them and others of their period. We also came to recognize that the omission of women from historical accounts of psychology placed a serious limitation on our understanding of the past and on women's sense of having a legitimate place in our discipline.

We wanted to retrieve our history. This quickly led us to work in the exciting area of women's history. We were interested in a privileged, elite group of women who had not yet come to the attention of women's historians and found that work in the sociology of science and social history also had particular relevance for our concerns. Our enthusiasm was fueled by two dominant elements: our appreciation of the significant role played by early women pioneers in opening to women the field we ourselves had entered and our conviction that our students and future generations of psychologists should learn of the early women.

Increasingly, we realized that many of the influences we were discovering in the lives of the early women are still potent today. We two have shared some of the experiences of the first generation, and our careers exemplify two of the patterns we identified in them: the sequential homemaking-professional career path and the combined family-professional career path. Elizabeth Scarborough (formerly Goodman) followed a college major in psychology with some graduate study in a cognate field, married, had two children, then returned to graduate study in psychology, receiving her Ph.D. sixteen years after college graduation. For five years she held sporadic part-time academic appointments before finally taking up full-time teaching at a state college. Laurel Furumoto, on the other hand, moved directly from college into a graduate program in psychology and marriage. The first of her two children was born before she completed her Ph.D. Immediately following graduate school she accepted an appointment at a women's college where she has remained.

Our collaboration has been greatly enriched by a network of professional colleagues who have been generous in their support and whose intellectual stimulation has been of immeasurable benefit. Especially important has been our association with the members of Cheiron (the International Society for the History of Behavioral and Social Sciences), the History of Psychology Division of the American Psychological Association, and the Wellesley Colloquium on the History of Psychology initiated by Larry Finison. Many, many persons in these groups have contributed both directly and indirectly to our work by their continuing encouragement, their friendship, and their examples of scholarly professionalism. We are especially grateful to Virginia Staudt Sexton, Michael M. Sokal, and Vicki P. Raeburn, who were particularly important in bringing this project into being.

We also especially appreciate the people who carefully read early drafts of the manuscript and shared with us their thoughtful critiques: Mary Roth Walsh, Leanna White Dunst, Ben Harris, Rebecca Mitchell, Christina Van Horn, and Natalie Golden. Barbara Kneubel's editorial evaluation was immensely important as we developed the manuscript.

As always in a work like ours, the assistance of archivists and librarians has been invaluable. We have included in our references a list of the archives we visited. We want to note the particular helpfulness of certain people: John Popplestone and Marion White McPherson of the Archives of the History of American Psychology, Kathleen Jacklin of Cornell University, Jane Knowles of Radcliffe College, and Earl Rogers of the University of Iowa. Staff members at the libraries of our home institutions provided innumerable services over the past several years. Special assistance has been given by Wilma Slaight at Wellesley and Margaret Pabst and Gary Barber at Fredonia. Thanks are due as well to the family of Mary Whiton Calkins who over the years have generously provided access to personal papers held by them.

Students too numerous to mention by name have helped the project along at various stages, from showing interest in our work to aiding in the research in concrete ways such as transcribing handwritten letters. The students in Laurel Furumoto's history seminar who did research papers on early women psychologists deserve special thanks for their contribution.

We are grateful also for the support of colleagues and administrators at Wellesley College and the State University of New York College at Fredonia. The coordination of our sabbatical leaves during the 1984-85 academic year made it possible for us to complete the manuscript. Earlier several small

xiv   PREFACE AND ACKNOWLEDGMENTS

grants supported our work as we gathered material: Furumoto received grants from the Brachman-Hoffman and Faculty Awards Programs at Wellesley College, and Scarborough was awarded a Faculty Research Fellowship and Grant-in-Aid by the State University of New York University Awards Program and a Fredonia Mini-Grant for Faculty Research.

UNTOLD LIVES:
THE FIRST GENERATION OF
AMERICAN WOMEN PSYCHOLOGISTS

Introduction

At the 1984 meeting of the American Psychological Association, we listened as a woman psychologist told an anecdote she offered as an example of the invisibility of the women in psychology's past. The incident was drawn from her own experience and dated back to the days when she was a student in a psychology course that dealt with the topic of perception. She recalled that among the classical theories covered in the course was one labeled the Ladd-Franklin theory of color vision, a theory that she assumed to be the work of Mr. Ladd and Mr. Franklin. Not until much later did she discover that the theory was, in fact, the contribution of a woman who after marriage used a hyphenated surname—Christine Ladd-Franklin.

This anecdote illustrates the way the presence of women psychologists has been blotted out of historical accounts of the discipline. In particular, courses and even the most recent textbooks in the history of psychology tend to perpetuate the myth of a womanless history, typically ignoring women psychologists and their contributions (Eberts and Gray 1982; Furumoto 1985; Goodman 1983).[1] This is more than a trivial historical oversight. Women have been an integral part of the discipline in the United States for almost one hundred years. Their participation began in the 1890s when psychology was just emerging as a science (Furumoto and Scarborough 1986).

Yet, despite their presence in psychology's past, women psychologists have been a well-kept secret in the history of the discipline. We argue that it is time to let that secret out.

Our aim in this book is to begin the task by providing an account of the lives of the first generation of American women psychologists.

HISTORICAL CONTEXT

To understand this first generation, it is necessary to know something of the lives of nineteenth-century women in the United States. It is also essential to have some grasp of the nature of the discipline of psychology which evolved as a science late in that century.

In the nineteenth century, Americans were obsessed with the idea of "woman's sphere," revealed in part by the torrent of prescriptive literature that appeared between 1820 and 1900 exhorting women to conform to a particular feminine role. A woman's life pattern in that period typically followed a straight and narrow path from childhood and upbringing in a family, through an apprenticeship in nurturing and domestic skills during adolescence, to marriage and motherhood (Cott 1977). Myriad published works exalted the virtues of "piety, purity, submissiveness, and domesticity" (Welter 1966:152) that women were expected to practice as they functioned within their sphere, the home, leaving men to attend to the duties of the wider world. It should be noted that these prescriptive writings were not directed at all American women, but primarily at northern white women of the middle and upper classes. The concept of woman's sphere was not seen as applying to women from other racial or class backgrounds.

This outpouring was an expression of "social norms formulated largely by men, outlining ideal types of female behavior" (Norton 1979:141). It prescribed how women were expected to conduct themselves rather than describing their actual behavior. In fact, the profusion of advice and prescriptive writing aimed at white women of the middle class may have gained its impetus from challenges to women's traditional role. These issued not only from women themselves but also from sweeping societal changes in progress—westward migration, industrialization, and urbanization.

In thinking about nineteenth-century women, then, we need to keep in mind a dual reality. While "women's ideal role was so sharply defined as to be oppressive" (Norton 1979:141), women were, in many respects, searching for autonomy. Manifestations of this can be seen in the founding of the women's rights movement, the growth of higher education for women, and the entry of women into the professions.

The Civil War provided an opportunity for women to make the push into higher education, which had previously been closed to them. Because of an overwhelming demand for labor, during the war women were allowed to step out of their domestic sphere to work in factories, on farms, as aides in hospitals and camps, and even as nurses and doctors. They also found places in the schools and colleges as teachers and students, establishing reputations in both roles. Thus women gained experience and developed new expectations. Further, they were supported in their quest for higher education by male abolitionists who "looked upon education as a reward for women's contributions in the war" (Solomon 1985:46).

The entry of women into higher education was accomplished over protest which from time to time shifted its grounds for opposition. For centuries popular opinion had questioned whether women were educable, and doubts lingered in the minds of many. At first even women who themselves passionately desired higher education were unsure about women's potential for intellectual achievement. One of the early women collegians, M. Carey Thomas, who later became president of Bryn Mawr College, said she could not remember a time when she was not sure "that studying and going to college were the things above all others" that she wished to do (Thomas 1908:64). Yet in her youth, uncertainty about women's capabilities plagued her, and she admitted, "I was always wondering whether it could be really true, as everyone thought, that boys were cleverer than girls."

As women began to enter the colleges in increasing numbers, they quickly proved their ability to compete intellectually in the academic arena. Fears then were raised about the negative consequences this would have for their health. In 1873 a book appeared by a former Harvard medical school professor, Dr. Edward H. Clarke, which set forth in gruesome detail the dire effects of higher education on women's physical well-being. The popular appeal of this work is underscored by the fact that within thirteen years the book went through seventeen editions. Clarke opposed all postpuberty education for women, arguing that it arrested the development of their reproductive systems. The end results of female education, he warned, would be "monstrous brains and puny bodies; abnormally active cerebration and abnormally weak digestion; flowing thought and constipated bowels" (quoted in Walsh 1977:126).

Another concern surfaced around the turn of the century as many observers pointed with alarm to statistics showing a declining rate of marriage and motherhood over the last decades of the nineteenth century for college educated women. Some educational authorities asserted that although the intellectual development of women was a desirable goal, their role as wives and mothers ought to take priority. The declining fertility of the woman college graduate excited fears that the very survival of the group to which she belonged, the white Protestant middle class, was in jeopardy (Caullery 1922: ch. 7). Commenting on this trend, psychologist G. Stanley Hall claimed that intellectually oriented women became "functionally castrated." According to Hall, not only did they abhor "the limitations of married life," but they were "incensed whenever attention is called to the functions peculiar to their sex" (Hall 1904:634).

Despite the protests, women entered higher education in ever increasing numbers and, in the latter decades of the century, established themselves on the academic scene. At about the same time, a proliferation of the professions was under way, and the social sciences, which included psychology, were beginning to emerge as disciplines within colleges and universities (Ross 1980). For those who aspired to professional status within the new fields, it became increasingly important to secure advanced, specialized training in the discipline they wished to enter. Graduate instruction, as we know it today with its emphasis on advanced course work and original research, made its appearance in the United States only relatively recently. It was an idea borrowed from the German university system and was first realized in America when the Johns Hopkins University opened in 1876. The excitement surrounding the Johns Hopkins experiment spurred Harvard to develop graduate offerings in the 1870s. And by the 1890s, several older schools such as Columbia, Yale, Cornell, and Michigan, as well as newly founded universities such as Chicago, Clark, and Stanford, had swelled the ranks of institutions promoting advanced instruction leading to the doctoral degree (Hawkins 1960; Veysey 1965).

Some of the young women who were in the vanguard of those acquiring college degrees set their sights on the advanced and specialized training offered in the new social science fields. Just as graduate education in psychology took shape in the United States in the 1890s, some of these women chose to enter the inchoate discipline. The routes of the early women who attempted to find a place for themselves in psychology were strewn with obstacles. First, they were venturing far beyond the limits of what was then seen as woman's proper sphere. Second, their gender excluded them from many of the institutions that offered the advanced work requisite to entering the field. Third, they were entering a new discipline that identified itself as a science. And the personal characteristics valued in a scientist included toughness, rigor, competitiveness, dominance, and rationality, hardly traits admired in a woman. Thus, "women scientists were . . . caught between two almost mutually exclusive stereotypes; as scientists they were atypical women; as women they were unusual scientists" (Rossiter 1982:xv).[2]

The early discipline of psychology was an enterprise vastly different from what it is today. Psychology is now commonly thought of as a profession mainly or even exclusively defined by the practice of psychotherapy, serving people who have emotional and behavioral disorders. This commonplace conception of psychology reflects the current predominance of clinicians within the field, but excludes other branches of the discipline.

The size and influence of the clinical branch of psychology is a relatively recent development stemming from the postwar needs of World War II veterans. Before the 1940s, psychology was primarily an academic, scientific discipline whose goal was to explain the workings of the mind and of behavior. To that end, psychologists in colleges and universities studied human and animal behavior, sensation and perception, learning, and cognition. While in the first half of the twentieth century there were psychologists interested in clinical, educational, and industrial applications of the science, their numbers and influence within the discipline remained limited until the clinical area experienced tremendous growth in the aftermath of World War II (see Napoli 1981; Sokal 1984).

The dual thrust of psychology, as both a science (acquiring knowledge) and an applied profession (using knowledge), has produced for psychology confusion in the use of the term professional. When applied to other sciences, "professional" refers to one who has met required training standards and is qualified to "practice" the science by conducting research and adding to its information base. More commonly and outside of scholarly fields, however, "professional" refers to a person who had met training standards, demonstrated competence, and is therefore qualified to practice by offering services to the public (as doctors and lawyers) or charging fees for the display of training and talent (as musicians and "pro" athletes). Academic psychologists best fit the first usage of "professional"; applied psychologists, the second. We use the term in its broadest sense, considering the profession of psychology to include both academic scientists and applied practitioners.

The profession that psychologists entered in the late nineteenth century, then, was a field populated by college and university professors. William James and Wilhelm Wundt have been credited with inaugurating the academic establishment of the new discipline in the 1870s at Harvard and Leipzig respectively, and G. Stanley Hall is commonly recognized for formally launching the new psychology in the United States at Johns Hopkins in the 1880s (Camfield 1973). The new psychology, also called "physiological psychology," identified itself as a laboratory science dedicated to investigating mental phenomena. Drawing its methods and inspiration from mid-nineteenth-century advances in physiology taking place in Germany, it attempted to distinguish itself from the older approach to psychology then represented in the college curriculum by courses in "mental philosophy." It accomplished this in part by presenting itself as a field based on experimentation rather than speculation (Hall 1887).

For more than a decade after the American Psychological Association (hereafter APA) was founded in 1892, American psychologists were intent upon establishing their field as a legitimate scientific profession. In this interval, several psychological journals were founded, and psychology made progress in academia as the number of laboratories increased and psychology became widespread in the curriculum. Also of crucial importance in this process was the organization of the APA itself, which provided recognition of psychology as a self-conscious emerging profession.[3]

From 1892 until 1906, during which time the APA grew from thirty-one to more than one hundred fifty members, the membership was quite heterogeneous. It included philosophers, educators, and physicians as well as those who could more appropriately be called "psychologists" by virtue of training and employment. Almost anyone expressing a desire to join was accepted, though the APA constitution of 1894 stipulated that "those are eligible for membership who are engaged in 'the advancement of Psychology as Science'" (Fernberger 1932:9).

During these formative years of the discipline, women comprised a larger proportion of workers in psychology than in the more mature sciences such as physics and chemistry. They were accepted as members of the APA apparently without dissent almost from its beginning. By the time the APA celebrated its twenty-fifth anniversary in 1917, women constituted 13 percent of the membership, and psychologist James McKeen Cattell (1917) noted that the percentage of women in the field surpassed that of any other science.[4]

Yet despite their relatively large numbers in the discipline, women's presence has been overlooked by historians reconstructing psychology's past. We must ask why. One explanation is that a womanless history of psychology is simply another example of the problematic absence or invisibility of women in historical accounts in general.

WOMEN'S HISTORY

In the last fifteen years or so, sparked by the women's movement of the 1960s, the field of women's history has emerged to address this problem. The work has been "undertaken by women who feel that their own past has been implicitly and mistakenly omitted in a history of humanity that is in fact a history of men" (Cott and Pleck 1979:9).

No hard and fast rules have yet emerged dictating how women's history should be written. Currently, a striking characteristic of the field is "the myriad ways in which [it] can be studied" (Berkin and Norton 1979:4). One of the leading advocates of women's history, American historian Gerda Lerner, has outlined three different approaches to the field (1979). Calling the first two "compensatory" and "contribution" history, she does not name the third, but describes it as an attempt to reconstruct women's experience. Compensatory history is, according to Lerner, the starting point for women's history. Using this approach, the historian searches the past for "lost" or overlooked women, rediscovering them to fill in the gaps. Lerner sees contribution history as the next task of women's history. In this approach a primary concern is women's participation in historical movements—for example, women's contributions to the abolition movement. Here, women are important or interesting only because of their impact on the movement, according to standards set by men.

Compensatory and contribution history answer the questions, "Who were the women in history?" and "What did they contribute?" While these approaches are necessary first steps in recovering women's lost past, they are not sufficient. Women as a group have a point of view, values, and experiences different from men's. These differences require a further necessary task for women's history—to reconstruct the past as it was experienced and understood by women. Lerner says to accomplish this task we must ask: "What would history be like if it were seen through the eyes of women and ordered by values they define?" (1979:178).

To see history "through the eyes of women" is important not only for the purpose of making historical accounts more complete. Women's history also has the potential to transform women's self understanding. Two women historians have described this process:

Women now seek to conform the study of history to its traditional purpose *par excellence:* to let us know where we have been, so that we will know where we are going. . . . Women who learn more fully about their own history often become more conscious of identification with their gender-group, more aware that their personal circumstances carry the legacy of a sex-specific historical experience, more determined to advance their position as women. (Cott and Pleck 1979:9)

Our book, which owes so much to the insights provided by recent work in women's history, in turn contributes to the field by reclaiming the untold lives of a particular group of professional women, the first generation to enter psychology in the United States.

DEFINITION OF GROUP

Who are the women we regard as the first generation? We have focused our study on the women identified as psychologists in *American Men of Science* (Cattell 1906), the first comprehensive directory of scientists in the United States.

Appearing early in the twentieth century, it was the project of a prominent early psychologist, James McKeen Cattell, whose goal was to provide a listing of every living individual in North America who had carried out scientific research.

Cattell cast a wide net in his attempt to identify all American scientists of the day, using among other means the membership lists of several national scientific societies, including the APA. He considered everyone who belonged to one of these groups qualified for inclusion in his directory. To be listed, an individual simply had to fill out and return an information blank provided by Cattell. Thus his criteria for inclusion, viewed by present standards, were not very selective. Cattell seemed to be more interested in compiling a comprehensive list of individuals who had some association with science, however tangential, than he was about weeding out people who didn't meet certain minimal specifications. Using this approach, he was able to come up with over four thousand entries for the directory, including approximately two hundred individuals who identified their scientific field as psychology.

Nineteen of these were women, and we include all of them as part of our first generation of women psychologists. Given the rather unsystematic method Cattell used in constructing the directory, a few of the women who appear were only tenuously related to psychology, while several early women who could be considered psychologists are not listed. For example, six women who had been admitted to the APA by 1906 were not in the first edition of *American Men of Science* (hereafter *AMS*). Recognizing the limitations of the directory, we chose to add these six women to our group.

Our selection was based therefore on two objective criteria: inclusion in the 1906 directory and membership in the APA by 1906. These criteria define a group of twenty-five who fairly represent the first generation of women in the field. Table 6.1 presents a list of these women and gives the dates of their entry into the field.

ORGANIZATION OF THE BOOK

The book is divided into two main sections which reflect Lerner's conceptualization of women's history, followed by a concluding chapter. The chapters in the first section attempt to reconstruct the past as it was experienced by women, Lerner's third approach. We accomplish this by focusing on themes that made the lives of the early women psychologists different from early men psychologists. These chapters illustrate what we hold to be an important truth: the historical reality of men and women has been different, or in other words, the past is gendered. The second section of the book undertakes compensatory and contribution history as well as a reconstruction of the experience of the entire group of women psychologists. Here we dismantle the myth, perpetuated by history of psychology courses and texts, that there have been no women in the history of the discipline.

Our approach in the five chapters that comprise the first section is to examine the past through the eyes of individual women psychologists. Each chapter tells the story of a woman whose life provides a vivid illustration of a particular gender-specific theme. Underlying the several themes in these chapters are two basic issues that are particularly relevant to women's lives: denial of opportunity (chapters 1, 4, and 5) and conflict between attachment and autonomy (chapters 2 and 3).

Chapter 1 concerns women's early attempts to secure graduate instruction in psychology, preparation that was essential to becoming a member of the profession. Here we portray the strategies used by Mary Whiton Calkins to circumvent the institutional barriers she encountered when she sought advanced study in psychology at Harvard in the early 1890s. There she successfully enlisted the aid of several sympathetic professors who joined her in contesting Harvard's policy of excluding women as graduate students. Although the professors with whom she studied praised her work highly and recommended she be awarded the Ph.D., Harvard stubbornly refused to grant the degree to a woman.

In the next chapter (chapter 2), we examine the bond between a middle-class daughter and her family during the late 1800s, emphasizing the family responsibilities that were part of her prescribed role. These duties, sometimes called "the family claim," form a central theme in the life story of Milicent W. Shinn, who grew up on her family's farm in California in the 1860s. After completing her doctorate at the University of California at Berkeley, just before the turn of the century, she returned to the family homestead, where she spent the rest of her life occupied with meeting her family obligations.

Chapter 3 takes up a wrenching dilemma confronting educated women in the late nineteenth century when social norms dictated that women must choose between marriage and career. This became a burning issue for Ethel Puffer, who completed her graduate studies in psychology at Harvard University in the 1890s and subsequently taught and published in the field until 1908. At that point she chose to marry, which ended her career in psychology but not her struggle with the marriage versus career dilemma.

In chapter 4 we consider how gender limited an early woman psychologist who chose to remain single and follow a career. Margaret Floy Washburn, the first woman to earn a doctorate in psychology, was highly regarded for her professional attainments and scientific contributions and was the second woman to be honored by election to the National Academy of Sciences. Yet she lived in an era when prestigious universities did not want women for their faculties. Washburn, despite her reputation, found her best opportunity for employment at Vassar College, an undergraduate college for women where her primary responsibility was teaching.

We take up the issue of the uncollegial treatment of women psychologists by their male peers in chapter 5, where we give an account of Christine Ladd-Franklin. After completing her graduate study at Johns Hopkins University in the early 1880s, she went on to become internationally recognized for her theory of color vision. In 1904 a society of psychologists was established by an eminent psychologist. The chapter relates the history of this society's ban on women members and how Ladd-Franklin challenged that policy.

In the second section of the book we move to compensatory and contribution history and develop a collective portrait of the early women psychologists. In addition to characterizing the group as a whole, we include cameos of several of the women in an appendix to highlight important dimensions of the experience of the women in this first generation. In chapter 6 we describe their origins, education, and life-styles; and in chapter 7 we document their careers and the contributions they made to psychology.

We conclude in chapter 8 by sketching the more recent history of women in psychology, commenting on changes in women's participation, their areas of specialization, their status in the discipline, and their experience as women in the profession. And finally we return to consider once again the question of why women have been excluded from psychology's history.

PART ONE

THE DIFFERENCE BEING
A WOMAN MADE

CHAPTER I

The Quest for Graduate Education:
Mary Calkins' Contest With Harvard University

Wellesley College had made a decision to introduce the new scientific psychology into its curriculum, and during the winter of 1888 a search was under way for a suitable candidate to fill the position. This women's college located sixteen miles west of Boston on the country estate of its founder, Henry Fowle Durant, had received its first students in 1875. Wellesley was from its beginning unusually committed to experimental science as a consequence of Durant's close friendship with Eben Horsford, a Harvard professor of chemistry who served as his trusted advisor.

Durant, originally a successful lawyer, underwent in the 1860s a conversion to evangelical Christianity that eventually led him to pour his energy and considerable resources into the cause of higher education for women. Unusual in his time, Durant believed in an all-women faculty as well as a woman president for the "college beautiful" he envisioned.[1] In 1874, when he faced the reality that he "could not find thirty learned women for college positions, he did a truly innovative thing: he found good teachers and paid for their training to do college work" (Horowitz 1984:54). So while it may seem odd to us today, it was not without precedent that Wellesley College, whose faculty had almost tripled in number by the late 1880s, would consider a woman with no training in psychology to fill the new post.[2] The person under consideration was a recently hired 25-year-old instructor who had shown initiative and effectiveness in her teaching as well as an interest in philosophy.

Mary Whiton Calkins had been hired on short notice in fall 1887 to fill an unexpected vacancy in the Greek Department. Just returned with her parents and three younger brothers from more than a year's sojourn in Europe, Calkins abandoned her plan to teach Greek to pupils on a private basis when she was offered the Wellesley appointment. Events followed in rapid order. Less than a week elapsed between the docking at Boston of the transatlantic steamer that carried the Calkins family and the day Calkins met her first class at Wellesley. Initially, she was exhilarated by the unanticipated opportunity to enter college teaching, but this quickly passed and she became seized with self-doubt. On the eve of her first day of teaching, her father wrote in his journal of his daughter's distress: "Thursday, Sept. 8 . . . Maidy has a great heart sinking that she is not equal to the work" (Wolcott Calkins' Log, CFP). And on the following day he observed: "She begins work, with sinking worse and worse." Once in the classroom, however, she found herself equal to the task and by Saturday her father wrote with obvious relief, "Maidy in better spirits after her second day at Wellesley."

Now, after having taught at the college for over a year, Calkins was facing another challenge, a shift from Greek to psychology. It was an idea that at first seemed so preposterous to her that she had difficulty in taking it seriously. However, with the support and encouragement of Mary Case, a professor in the Philosophy Department, she began to consider what kind of preparation she would need if she were offered the new position. Still undecided and somewhat hesitant about whether she should accept such an offer, she sought advice from some of her former professors at Smith College. Three years earlier she had received her B.A. with a concentration in the classics from this women's college in western Massachusetts which had opened its doors in the same year as Wellesley.

Calkins wrote first to her much admired English instructor, Mary Augusta Jordan, a young woman who had begun her

Mary Whiton Calkins as a young faculty member at Wellesley College, 1889. (Courtesy of the Wellesley College Archives.)

Mary S. Case (seated front row facing right), faculty member who was a mentor to Mary W. Calkins, and students who took their meals at her table in the College Hall dining room shown on the steps of College Hall, 1885. (Courtesy of the Wellesley College Archives.)

Wellesley College Tree Day, 1887. This ceremony took place annually in late May and was one of the big events of the year. It featured addresses and songs by the freshman class and culminated in members of that class planting a tree. The main building, College Hall, is in the background. (Courtesy of the Wellesley College Archives.)

career in college teaching without graduate study. Jordan advised Calkins to "be bold" and accept the position if it were offered (undated letter, MWCP). In Jordan's opinion, "special preparation [could] well afford to wait."

Calkins also wrote to Charles Edward Garman. In her senior year, she had taken a course from him that was in the tradition of the older speculative and philosophical approach to psychology. By the closing years of the nineteenth century, this kind of course, typically having strong religious overtones, was being replaced in college curricula by a scientific approach to the subject called "the new psychology." Though she looked to her former teacher for guidance, Calkins would ultimately embark on study rooted in this newer approach. Calkins sought Garman's opinion on whether anyone should consider teaching psychology without "thorough and long preparation" (January 1, 1889, CEGP). She explained that she had not done any further study in the subject since she had taken psychology with him in her senior year. Her only additional preparation was some reading she had done on her own that had increased her interest in psychology. "Admitting an antecedent enthusiasm for the subject," she asked him if he thought it possible "that anyone with such insufficient preparation can properly teach a class?" In his reply, Garman agreed with Jordan and encouraged Calkins to accept the position if it was offered. He saw in his former student "natural qualifications" for teaching psychology and predicted that she "would be eminently successful" at it (April 27, 1889, MWCP).

For a time, Calkins was allowed to postpone deciding about the position in psychology. That spring she was told that she was needed in the Greek Department for at least another academic year. By summer, however, she seems to have settled the matter in her own mind. Writing to Garman about the change in plans, she expressed definite aspirations to enter the new field, saying that she hoped she might "sometime be able to study and to teach psychology" (June 1, 1889, CEGP).

Her hope materialized during the following academic year: Calkins was offered the position of instructor in psychology, which she accepted. The matter of special preparation was decided for her by the president of Wellesley, who stipulated that the appointment was contingent upon Calkins' completing a full year of study in psychology.

The question then confronting Calkins was where and how to spend her year of preparation. Turning again to Garman, in an ardent letter she urged him to let her spend at least some part of her year with him. She had positively decided on only two things, she told him: "First . . . I wish and need to study with you . . . second, that some part of my work must be in the line of physiological psychology" (February 22, 1890, CEGP).[3] Feeling presumptuous in asking Garman to direct her work, she hastened to give him her reasons: "I owe to you so much of my interest in psychology, my understanding of the subject, any apprehension of its relation to the great life problems, that your personal help seems to me almost necessary, if I am to enter on work of such importance." She asked him if he were planning to be at home in Amherst that summer or if she could bring her books and spend a few weeks with him in the place where he would vacation. Admitting, "It might not be a very restful retreat, if I invaded it," she added, "but I should try to be an exhilarating student."

It was more than two months before Garman replied, explaining that illness and overwork during the winter made it absolutely necessary for him to have a complete change from mental activity in the summer months. His letter made it plain that Calkins could not entertain any hope of beginning her study of psychology that summer with Garman (April 18, 1890, MWCP).

Compelled to look beyond her former teacher for instruction, Calkins began to explore the opportunities for women in European as well as American universities. In 1890 an American who wanted to study the new scientific psychology was likely to go abroad to Germany where there were several active psychological laboratories.[4] Both Garman and H. N. Gardiner, her philosophy professor at Smith, praised the German universities. However, they acknowledged that as a woman, Calkins could expect to encounter difficulty in getting access to the instruction she sought. Gardiner wrote "Germany is a good place to study. . . . Whether you could have the privilege of attending lectures or obtaining private instruction in Psychology and Philosophy at any of the German universities outside of Zürich, I do not know" (May 1, 1890, MWCP). And Garman commented that he would recommend that she study in Germany "if ladies [were] allowed the same privileges as men" (April 28, 1890, MWCP).

The concerns expressed by her former professors were well founded. Letters and published accounts describing the experiences of American women who made an attempt to study at German universities in the nineteenth century speak of restrictions, frustration, and the peremptory attitudes of many university officials and professors toward women. One writer, in a letter to the editor of *The Nation,* referred to the "bitter experiences . . . trials and disappointments" that American women were obliged to undergo during the 1890s in their efforts to obtain admission at the University of Leipzig ("Pioneer Women Students in Germany," 1897).[5]

A letter Mary Calkins received in the summer of 1890 gave her a firsthand account of the predicament of women at another of the German universities. The writer offered Calkins her opinion about a woman's chances to study at the University of Göttingen: "I wish I might encourage you; but past experience has proved to me the utter uselessness of trying to enlighten the authorities,—at least in our generation" (M. L. Perrin to Calkins, July 12, 1890, MWCP). Describing the situation, she reported that in her last year there "a lady tried every possible means of gaining access to lectures. . . . Finally she succeeded in persuading one of the Professors to give her private lessons." The letter concluded with a bitter comment revealing the negative impact on women of institutional restrictions abroad, which were compounded by bad treatment at the hands of individual professors: "If you wish to study under a certain Prof. I think he would for a nominal price think it rather a joke to give you lessons."

It is not clear how heavily the unfavorable situation reported for women weighed in Calkins' decision not to study in Germany. There is evidence that indicates she had received permission to attend Wilhelm Wundt's lectures at Leipzig. But in the spring and summer of 1890 she was also exploring possibilities for advanced work in psychology closer to home. At that time, laboratories in America devoted to the new psychology were few enough to be counted on the fingers of both hands, and most of them were in their infancy. Only the facilities at Harvard and at Johns Hopkins were established prior to 1887. By 1889, however, laboratories had been set up at six other institutions—Indiana, Pennsylvania, Wisconsin, Clark, Kansas, and Nebraska.

It was not only work in scientific psychology that was new and offered by very few institutions; graduate study in general was just becoming established in the United States. In fact, the period from 1876 to 1890 has been called the "adolescence of the American universities" (James 1930:3). Before Johns Hopkins opened in 1876 post-baccalaureate training, a hallmark of the university, only tentatively and sporadically appeared in institutions devoted to higher education in the United States. In the next fifteen years, Hopkins along with Harvard led the way in developing programs of graduate study, and by 1890 several other universities had joined the effort. There were only 389 students enrolled in graduate work in the United States in 1876. By 1890 the number had grown to 3,382 and included 409 women. For the first time, American students could find in the United States advanced training comparable to Europe.[6]

The University of Michigan and Yale were among the institutions that by 1890 were offering some graduate instruction in psychology, and Calkins investigated both. She wrote to John Dewey at Michigan in spring 1890 to inquire what psychology courses would be taught there the following year. In a very cordial reply he outlined the tentative curriculum and noted the lack of a laboratory for the course in physiological psychology. At Yale the situation for psychology was similar, as reported by one of Calkins' classmates from Smith College, Anna Alice Cutler, who was pursuing graduate study there. Yale, however, unlike Michigan, which admitted women to graduate study on an equal basis with men, was still placing restrictions on women seeking advanced work.

When on Calkins' behalf Cutler consulted G. T. Ladd, the professor of psychology at Yale, about courses open to a woman who wanted to study psychology in order to teach, he felt at liberty to give permission for entering only some of his courses. He was reluctant, for example, to admit a woman to his physiological psychology course before consulting the institutional authorities. Ladd had Cutler relay a message to Calkins that he had been able to obtain official sanction for her to attend this course as a guest but not as a regular student. Cutler wryly commented on the limitations of this arrangement. As she informed her friend, because it was an undergraduate course, technically closed to women, "you could open your mouth only after decree of the Faculty & Corporation" (June 5, 1890, MWCP). Cutler added that the situation of women students was better in the graduate courses where "you can take as full a part . . . as you choose."

Although Cutler was not very enthusiastic about either the courses she was taking or her professors at Yale, she urged Calkins to join her there. Her reason seems to lie in the fact that she felt terribly lonely in that exclusively male setting. She confided, "Personally I should be immensely glad if you would come. We might be able to get some delightful work together. . . . If there were only one or two other girls who would come to join us we could get a tremendous amount" (May 28, 1890, MWCP). Cutler's letters to Calkins speak poignantly of the restrictions and social isolation experienced by the early women graduate students at Yale and elsewhere at institutions that barely tolerated their presence.

It is clear that Calkins could have studied at Michigan with Dewey or at Yale with Ladd. That she chose to do neither could be attributed to the fact that these institutions could not offer her work in a psychological laboratory—and instituting psychology at Wellesley would involve setting up a laboratory if the new psychology were to be properly introduced. There were, however, two institutions close at hand that were among the few in America to have laboratories in operation by 1890. And, they had the added advantage of being near enough to allow Calkins to remain with her family while she studied. It was to these universities—Harvard and Clark—that she turned for her year of advanced work; however, neither institution was open at that time to women students.

At Harvard the authorities, alumni, and students were almost to a man adamantly opposed to the idea of coeducation. The prevalent attitude toward including women as students was akin to that toward including certain ethnic minorities. To have women students at Harvard would signal institutional decay (Hawkins 1972: ch. 6). By the 1870s, however, there was increasing pressure from groups in Boston and Cambridge to open the educational opportunities of Harvard to young women. Wives, sisters, and daughters of Harvard alumni and faculty joined with educational reformers in demanding access. A compromise, which avoided coeducation and at the same time provided a way for Harvard professors to augment their meager salaries, was an arrangement that came to be called the "Harvard Annex."

Mary Calkins' first approach to Harvard was by way of the "Annex." In reality the Annex had no official relationship to Harvard. Rather, it was a system whereby Harvard faculty members offered courses on a private basis to classes of women students. Initiated in 1879, the instruction usually consisted of a repetition of courses given at Harvard.[7] In May 1890 Calkins contacted Josiah Royce, a professor in the Harvard Philosophy Department, to inquire about courses he planned to offer in the Annex in the coming year and to request an interview. Her meeting with him resulted in a proposal: that instead of taking courses in the Annex, she do regular advanced work in psychology and philosophy by attending the seminars given by him and William James.[8]

It is not clear who initially suggested that Calkins study at Harvard proper rather than the Annex, but both James and Royce enthusiastically supported this plan. Royce acknowledged that the instruction he could offer Calkins in the Annex "would be of course unequal to a regular advanced course" (May 27, 1890, MWCP). And James did not offer any courses in the Annex. It also happened that another Harvard philosopher, George Herbert Palmer, had recently married

William James (1842–1910). (Courtesy of the Harvard University Archives.)

Alice Freeman, the former president of Wellesley College. Freeman had hired Calkins three years earlier to teach at Wellesley, and both she and her husband described Calkins to James as "a woman of exceptional intellectual capacity" (James to C. W. Eliot, May 23, 1890, CWEPP).

The proposal that Calkins attend the Harvard seminars of James and Royce was no sooner formulated than it ran into stiff opposition from Harvard president Charles W. Eliot, who had to be consulted about the arrangement. Eliot personally was a champion of the view that men and women should be educated separately, each according to their, in his view, differing natures. Furthermore, Eliot was accountable to the policy-setting and decision-making bodies at Harvard—the Corporation and the Overseers—both of which emphatically opposed any move toward coeducation. Eliot did not approve the plan for Calkins, as James informed her at the end of May:

It seems very hard. But he has to keep guard all along the line, and I suppose that laxity would soon produce an involuntary and unintended occupation of a great many of these higher courses by women. . . . Believe in my sincere regret for this action of our authorities. (May 24, 1890, MWCP)

Royce also wrote to Calkins expressing his perplexity over Eliot's refusal and his regret that he and James would not be allowed to let her attend their seminars: "I regard this official view as one of the mysteries which no one may hope to penetrate who is not himself accustomed to the executive point of outlook" (May 27, 1890, MWCP).

Apparently William James was not willing to let the matter drop despite Eliot's negative decision. Five days after his first letter, he sent Calkins another indicating that he had tried to persuade the president to change his mind without success. James, in defense of Eliot, explained that the president had a few years earlier received a stern rebuke from the Harvard Overseers, who were very sensitive on the issue of coeducation, "for winking at just this thing." And as a consequence,

James told Calkins, "he is forced now to be strict" (May 29, n.y., MWCP).

In June, just after this exchange of letters, two of Mary Calkins' younger brothers, Leighton and Raymond, were among the nearly 300 young men who were awarded bachelor's degrees at the commencement ceremony for the Harvard class of 1890. The following day her father had an interview with President Eliot to plead his daughter's case. A man of about sixty, three years Eliot's senior, the Reverend Wolcott Calkins was a well-known evangelical minister. Strong willed and remarkably vigorous, physically as well as intellectually, he was described by his youngest son Grosvenor as "planning and pulling wires for the advantage, in his opinion, of his children" (Grosvenor Calkins, Memoirs, CFP). Mary Calkins, his eldest child, was on more than one occasion the object of such paternal solicitude.

His wife Charlotte had once described her husband as "unconventional." Perhaps this trait helped foster his daughter's nontraditional aspirations for advanced academic training. Wolcott seemed inclined to encourage his bright, young daughter to explore activities beyond those customarily thought to be appropriate for others of her gender. For example, when she was just a toddler, her father took her with him on excursions, riding horseback. Much later, when she brought a college friend home for the holidays, her father had both of them up on ladders puttying the thousands of nail holes in the woodwork of their new house. And on the family's transatlantic voyage, in a stiff gale, her father had escorted his daughter to the stairs of the bridge. There, he noted approvingly, "as the wind was steadily increasing . . . she clung and enjoyed greatly the tremendous pitching" (Wolcott Calkins' Log, August 1887, CFP).

Though of different backgrounds and educational attainments, both of Mary Calkins' parents valued intellectual pursuits. Both were intimately involved in directing the education of their children, sons and daughters alike. Wolcott had been born on a farm in western New York, the eighth of nine children. From the time of his father's death when Wolcott was sixteen, he supported himself, teaching for several years to save enough money to pay for his college expenses at Yale from which he graduated in 1856. Studying first for a year at Union Theological Seminary and later in Germany at the University of Halle for two years, he was ordained as a Congregational minister in 1862.

Just prior to leaving for Germany, in June 1860, Wolcott married a 20-year-old Bostonian, daughter of an established New England Puritan family. His bride, Charlotte Grosvenor Whiton, was an intelligent, sensitive young woman with a strong interest in music. She had received tutoring in voice and piano, but the rest of her formal education, typical of women who grew up before the Civil War, was limited compared to her husband's and stopped far short of work at the college level.

Wolcott Calkins held brief pastorates upon the couple's return from Germany, first in Hartford, Connecticut, where Mary Calkins was born in 1863, and then in Philadelphia. In 1866 he accepted a post as a pastor of a Presbyterian church in Buffalo, New York, where he remained for fourteen years. There Mary grew up enjoying a very close relationship with her slightly younger sister Maud. Three brothers who were considerably younger did not provide their elder sisters with much companionship, although the brothers were the beneficiaries of Mary's tutoring.

From the time she was a little girl, in addition to Maud, Mary had another constant comrade, Sophie Jewett. Sophie's parents died when she was very young, and thereafter she had been welcomed into the family of her minister, Wolcott Calkins, whose home she called her "second home." Mary Calkins fondly remembered the fine times she and Sophie had together as little girls in her father's study: "The two children discussed grave mysteries or bent together over books in strange tongues, though ever ready to be lured from the deep window seat to range the house or to climb the church belfry" (Jewett and Calkins 1910, viii).

Their childhood companioning grew into a lifelong friendship. Sophie Jewett joined the faculty at Wellesley College in English literature in 1889, just two years after Mary began teaching there. The two women remained beloved friends and colleagues at Wellesley for twenty years, until Sophie's untimely death after an operation for appendicitis when she was forty-eight years old.

During the time Mary Calkins was growing up in Buffalo, when she was about ten years old, a crisis occurred that was to have a lasting impact on the family. Charlotte Calkins' health gave way under the prolonged strain of nursing her children through a series of grave childhood illnesses. Experiencing a complete emotional and physical collapse, she was dangerously ill for more than two years and remained in delicate health for the rest of her life. Over the years Mary came to assume a strongly protective stance toward her mother, and throughout her life providing companionship to her mother and assuring her well-being was one of her primary concerns.

The Calkins family left Buffalo for Massachusetts in 1880 when Wolcott accepted the call of a Congregational church in the city of Newton, located a few miles west of Boston. In Newton he designed and supervised the construction of a house for his family, the house in which Mary was to spend her entire adult life. Shortly after their move, the family was jarred by tragedy. Maud developed rheumatic heart disease and died during her sister Mary's freshman year at Smith College. With Maud's death Mary became the family's sole surviving daughter. As her brothers married and moved away from home and her parents grew older, ever sensitive to her familial obligations, Mary Calkins assumed more and more responsibility for running the household and looking after her parents' welfare. These duties were to occupy her throughout her life—she outlived her father by only six years and she was survived by her mother.

A record of the meeting that took place between Wolcott Calkins and President Eliot in June 1890 to discuss the ambition of the minister's daughter to study at Harvard survives in the pages of Wolcott's journal. He noted that Eliot began the interview by congratulating him on the "substantial success" of his sons and expressed his surprise "that he knows so much about them" (Wolcott Calkins' Log, CFP). The entry continued: "Then came my request that Maidy might pursue her philosophical course with [James and Royce] next year. Favorably received, but must come before the Corporation." A few days later he wrote, "Nearly all day on the letter to the Corporation of Harvard about Maidy. Close work." The resulting petition, dated July 1, 1890, was submitted to the Corporation accompanied by a letter of support from the president of Wellesley College. A lengthy document, the petition meticulously spelled out the facts of the case and attempted to reassure the Corporation that granting this request would not provide an embarrassing precedent that could be used in arguments for coeducation at Harvard. What was being asked was "postgraduate and professional instruction for one who is already a member of a college faculty." Finally, the petition concluded, there was no university where she could "find a course of study so exactly suited to her present needs . . . where she can live in her own home, and attend seminary (*sic*) courses in small classes of advanced students, meeting only in the parlors of the instructors, where a lady may be received with propriety" (CWEPP).

That summer Mary Calkins received warm and encouraging notes from both James and Royce. They seemed optimistic that the Corporation would approve the petition, and James expressed his indignation with Harvard's exclusionary policy: "It is flagitious that you should be kept out. —Enough to make dynamiters of you and all women. I hope and trust that your application will break the barrier" (July 30, 1890, MWCP).

Although the arguments in Wolcott Calkins' petition to the Harvard Corporation did not succeed in breaking the barrier, they at least were persuasive enough to provide an entering wedge. On October 1 the Corporation voted to authorize James and Royce to permit Mary Calkins "to attend gratu-

Mary Whiton Calkins (1863–1930). (Courtesy of the Wellesley College Archives.)

itously their courses in psychology and Hegel respectively during the current academic year." So that there would be no misunderstanding about the issue of coeducation at Harvard, the Corporation specified that "by accepting this privilege Miss Calkins does not become a student of the University entitled to registration" (CR).

Two days after the vote, James wrote Calkins, welcoming her into his seminar. That spring he had completed and sent off to his publisher a project that had occupied him for twelve years. *The Principles of Psychology,* a two-volume, 1400-page work that was to take its place as a classic in the field, appeared in the fall of 1890. James indicated in his letter, in rather vague terms, the plan for the psychology seminar that she was to attend: "My students four in number seem of divergent tendencies and I don't know just what will come of the course. Having published my two rather fat tomes, I shan't lecture, but the thing will probably resolve itself into advice and possibly some experimentation." James concluded his letter by cordially inviting her to come early to the next meeting of the seminar "so as to have a little talk in advance . . . and take tea" (October 3, 1890, MWCP). One can only conjecture whether this gracious gesture was prompted solely by a spirit of hospitality or also by some uneasiness on James' part about the unorthodoxy of including a woman in a Harvard seminar.

James' lectures have been described as conversational, and he is said to have approached his students as equals rather than as inferiors (Veysey 1965:228–29). While his spontaneous and direct manner proved disconcerting to some students and produced lectures that were uneven, he made a lasting impression on many students, and Calkins was among them. In an autobiographical account written almost forty years later, she described her experience in James' seminar, where she remembered gaining "beyond all else, a vivid sense of the concreteness of psychology." Looking back on it, she recalled:

I began the serious study of psychology with William James. Most unhappily for them and most fortunately for me the other members of his seminary in psychology dropped away in the early weeks of the fall of 1890; and James and I were left . . . at either side of a library fire. *The Principles of Psychology* was warm from the press; and my absorbed study of those brilliant, erudite, and provocative volumes, as interpreted by their writer, was my introduction to psychology. (Calkins 1930:31)

Thus despite all the obstacles placed in her path, Mary Calkins made her entry into psychology in an impressive manner, tutored by a man many consider psychology's most revered founder. Why all of the other students dropped out of the seminar invites speculation. Harvard men in that era were expressing genuine alarm in their student newspaper regarding the possible intrusion of women into their laboratories and classrooms. It is just possible that Calkins' presence in James' seminar quite literally drove the men students out.

Living with her parents and youngest brother in the family home in Newton, she traveled by streetcar ten miles east to Cambridge to attend the seminars at Harvard. And during the same year, she traveled forty miles west to Worcester for laboratory work at Clark University. At a time when it appeared unlikely that Calkins would be able to study at Harvard, James had suggested that she consider instead the recently founded Clark University, where G. Stanley Hall was president. Hall, along with James, was an early influential figure in scientific psychology, and James had written Calkins, "Stanley Hall's Psychological department ought to be the best in the world" (May 24, 1890, MWCP).

Mary Calkins did look to Clark for instruction in the fall of 1890 just one year after it had opened. It was her good fortune there to become the private student of Edmund C. Sanford. Just three years older than Calkins, he had come to Clark the previous year after completing his Ph.D. at Johns Hopkins. Described by his cousin Milicent Shinn as a "thoroughly good and sweet" person (Milicent Shinn to Daniel C. Gilman, June 5, 1890, DCGP), Sanford was also remembered fondly by

Edmund C. Sanford (1859–1924). (Courtesy of the Clark University Archives.)

Calkins. In her autobiography Calkins referred to him as "a teacher unrivalled for the richness and precision of his knowledge of experimental procedure and for the prodigality with which he lavished time and interest upon his students" (Calkins 1930:32).

Clark University did not take the step of officially admitting women as students until 1900. Prior to this, if women wished to take advantage of the graduate instruction available at this new research-oriented university, they were compelled to make special arrangements with individual instructors. Explaining Clark's stance just before it opened, G. Stanley Hall told Christine Ladd-Franklin that "the question of admitting women [was] about to be settled adversely on account of the fact that no applications from women [had] been received" (C. Ladd-Franklin to M. C. Thomas, May 18, 1889, CLF&FFP). Ladd-Franklin was quick to point out that this was a "foolish reason." It is difficult to know how much credence to give Hall's explanation. As his biographer points out, both his personal relationships and his ideas were characterized by duplicity (Ross 1972:xv). The real reason for exclusion may have been that the new university's benefactor, Jonas Clark, objected to admitting women (219).

In any case, Calkins had no reason to hope that she could enter Clark on a regular basis and was obliged to learn laboratory psychology by arranging to take private lessons from Sanford. In addition to training her in the detail of laboratory experiments, Sanford collaborated with Calkins on a study in which they recorded the contents of their dreams over a seven-week period. He subsequently presented the results of their research at the first annual meeting of the American Psychological Association in December 1892. Sanford also served as a consultant to Calkins when she set up a laboratory at Wellesley in fall 1891. He wrote to her on several occasions discussing in great detail a range of issues related to getting the psychological work under way.

William James, too, served as her instructor and consultant even after the seminar ended. In January 1891 he invited Calkins

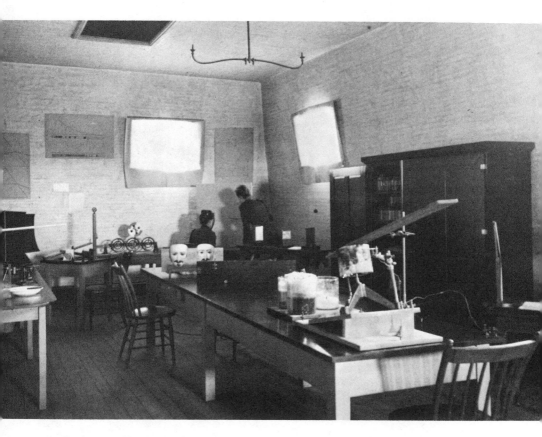

Wellesley College Psychological Laboratory on the top floor of College Hall, 1890s. (Courtesy of the Wellesley College Archives.)

to join him in his laboratory for a demonstration of how to dissect sheep's brains and later gave her advice about appropriate containers for storing brains. When he read the paper she had written for him on the topic of association of ideas, he said it had given him "exquisite delight" and encouraged her to publish it, adding that if she were too modest he would bring it to the attention of the editor of the appropriate journal himself (August 12, 1891 and November 6, 1891, MWCP). In subsequent correspondence James offered her suggestions on revising

The Agora Society, Wellesley College, 1897. A group composed of students and faculty that met to discuss social and political issues of the day. Mary Calkins is in the front row (fourth from the right, facing left), and Frances Rousmaniere (see chapter 7 and cameo in appendix A) is in the second row (third from the left). (Courtesy of the Wellesley College Archives.)

the paper; Calkins remembered it as her "first published contribution to psychology" (Calkins 1930:33).

In fall 1891 Calkins returned to Wellesley to begin her new work in psychology and establish a laboratory—the first in a women's college—to be used in conjunction with her teaching. Barely a semester had elapsed, however, before she began corresponding with her teachers of the previous year about opportunities for further study in psychology. A laboratory had recently opened at Cornell University, and Royce endorsed her idea of going there if she could get a fellowship. He also advised her not to postpone her plans for additional preparation, telling Calkins: "Your work will be aided by another year of study taken pretty early" (February 17, 1892, MWCP). Cornell had long admitted women to its graduate programs and, even more unusual for universities at the time, considered women as candidates for fellowships (Conable 1977:85–86).

Sanford, on the other hand, thought she would be better off studying in Europe, insisting that the opportunities for women there were increasing at a faster pace than they were in the United States. Furthermore, he asserted that a European Ph.D. was more prestigious than an American one, confiding to her, "I don't think that my J.[ohns] H.[opkins] U.[niversity] Ph.D. is quite so impressive to the average person in authority as a Leipzig one would be" (February 16, 1892, MWCP). Convinced that Calkins was unduly pessimistic about the opportunities for women in Europe, he told her that on a recent visit to Harvard he had seen "a picture of Münsterberg and his Seminary (*sic*)—amongst the rest a lady!" Sanford then contrasted the increasing acceptance of women as students in European universities with the situation in the United States exclaiming: "They are beginning to wake up over there, the more shame to Johns Hopkins and Clark—an ineffable shame that you can't get a fellowship in your own country in institutions given to advanced work."

James, writing to Calkins at about the same time, confirmed Sanford's speculation about Münsterberg, a young German psychologist at the University of Freiburg and a former student of Wundt at Leipzig. He indicated that Münsterberg had indeed included a woman in his seminar the previous year, the woman Sanford had noticed in the photograph. But James was mysteriously insistent in imploring Calkins to delay as long as possible deciding where to study the following year. His reason soon became clear: Münsterberg was coming to Harvard. James advised Calkins in April 1892: "With regard to M-berg, you may disclose the awful secret now, since the Corporation has regularly appointed him" (April 29, 1892, MWCP).

William James had first met Hugo Münsterberg in 1889 at the International Congress of Physiological Psychology and had corresponded with him subsequently. James thought highly of Münsterberg's work and had orchestrated the plan to bring Münsterberg to Harvard to head the psychological laboratory. At a time when Germany's influence on American higher education was at its height, Münsterberg's decision for Harvard represented a coup (Hale 1980:46).

So, instead of asking admission to his Freiburg laboratory as she had planned, Calkins found herself returning to Harvard where Münsterberg began a three-year appointment in fall 1892. This time, Calkins herself drafted a petition to present to the Harvard authorities requesting to work with Münsterberg in the psychological laboratory. Describing the work she had completed with James and Sanford, she went on to explain "I am now in great need of further direction, and in especial need of good laboratory opportunities" (to President and Corporation, December 30, 1892, CWEPP).

Münsterberg sent a letter supporting her petition, taking pains to indicate that Calkins would be suitably segregated from the men students working in the laboratory and, as well, chaperoned by Münsterberg himself. This was no doubt intended to allay any anxieties of the authorities about the co-educational aspect of the situation: "The investigations can be so arranged that Miss Calkins works in a special room of the laboratory with my continual personal assistance" (to the President and Fellows of Harvard College, January 3, 1893, CWEPP). Again refusing to grant regular student status to Calkins, the Corporation decided that she would be "welcome to attend the instruction of Professor Münsterberg in his laboratory as a guest; but not as a registered student of the University" (C. W. Eliot to Madam, January 9, 1893, MWCP).

Münsterberg would be Calkins' teacher, mentor, and advocate for many years to come. Just the same age—Calkins was two months older than he—they also shared a deep appreciation of German language, scholarship, and culture. This appreciation had been cultivated in Calkins by her parents, who had become fluent in the language during the two years they had spent in Germany immediately following their marriage. Wolcott Calkins insisted that only German be spoken in the household when their firstborn, Maidy, was learning to talk. Both parents noted with obvious delight the result of this experiment: their tiny daughter's facility in German—her first language.

Calkins and Münsterberg also shared traditional views of the family and women's role in it. Calkins, for example, could not entertain the idea that a woman might decline marriage in order to follow a career. She expressed this view quite clearly in her notes for an address she gave when she was about fifty: "I should pity and condemn the woman (if there could be such a woman) who turned aside from marriage with a good man whose love she returned in order to pursue any end of the scholar" (Place of Scholarship in Life, 1913, MWCP). She herself had a lifelong academic career and never married. Taking her words at face value leads one to conclude that she was never confronted with the necessity to choose between a desirable marriage offer and her scholarly career.

A few years after expressing the view that for women the possibility of entering into a good marriage should take precedence over a career, Calkins explicitly rejected the label of "feminist" during an interview for a newspaper. In an article announcing her arrival as a visiting professor at the University of California at Berkeley, she admitted to being a suffragist but denied being a feminist. The reason she offered for dissociating herself from this movement was linked with her positive view of the traditional family: "Wherein feminism makes encroachments into the institution of the family, I cannot follow it" (Scrapbook, MWCP).

Münsterberg held to the conventional German view that women had an obligation to society that made it necessary for them to put aside personal ambitions in favor of producing and nurturing the next generation. However, he also believed that there were a few "exceptional women of special talent" who could be exempted from the motherhood mandate to pursue careers (Münsterberg 1901:627). No doubt Münsterberg considered Calkins to be such a woman.

Early in 1893 Calkins began work in Münsterberg's laboratory, work she was to continue for the next year and a half while fulfilling regular teaching responsibilities at Wellesley. Then, in the 1894–95 academic year, she took a leave from the college to devote herself full-time to the laboratory. In her autobiography she described this period of her life in glowing terms as a time of intellectual flourishing under Münsterberg's "inspiring direction" in an environment where she felt completely accepted. Although the location of the psychological laboratory was not ideal, situated as it was "within hearing on the one side of the hand-organs and the street-car bells of Harvard Square and on the other of the often vociferous outbursts of Professor Copeland's 'elocution' classes," for Calkins "it was nonetheless the scene of absorbing work" (Calkins 1930:33). Observing that "the unprecedented incursion of a woman might well have been resented" (34) she expressed her gratitude for the unusually supportive atmosphere she found there. Not only had Münsterberg "swung the laboratory doors open" to her, but she also remembered receiving a "friendly, comradely, and refreshingly matter-of-fact welcome" from the men assistants and students (33–34).

While Calkins was carrying out her research, an original investigation of factors influencing memory, Münsterberg sent a letter to the Harvard Corporation asking whether she could be admitted as a candidate for the Ph.D.[9] He described her in superlatives as the strongest of all the students who had worked in the laboratory since he had been at Harvard and as "superior also to all candidates of the philosophical Ph.D. during the last years" (to President and Fellows of Harvard College, October 23, 1894, CWEPP). He added: "More than that: she is surely one of the strongest professors of psychology in the country." Münsterberg ended his appeal with the bold assertion that "the Harvard Ph.D. attached to the name of Mary W. Calkins would mean not only a well deserved honor for her, but above all an honor for the philosophical department of Harvard University." The Corporation did not agree; their records reveal that Münsterberg's "request was considered, and refused" (October 29, 1894, CR).

The timing of Münsterberg's request to the Corporation, coming just a few months after Harvard had "authorized the admission of 'properly qualified women' to courses designed 'primarily for graduates' " (Woody 1929 2:336), can be seen as an attempt to ascertain whether women could hope that their graduate work would earn a degree. Although the university was now willing to admit women to graduate instruction on a regular basis, it remained unwilling to consider their work as leading to the Harvard Ph.D. The question of what degree should be awarded to women who completed all work for the Ph.D. in Harvard graduate departments would remain a hotly debated issue for the next several years.

In spring 1895, just as Münsterberg's three-year appointment at Harvard was ending and he was planning to return to Germany, Calkins asked the Philosophy Department to give her an unofficial examination. The department agreed, and Royce, at that time department chair, informed her that she would be given "an informal examination, equivalent, in its nature and methods, to the regular examination for the Degree of Doctor of Philosophy" (April 11, 1895, MWCP). The outcome of the examination conducted in May by the professors of the Philosophy Department was formally reported to the Harvard authorities by Royce. Not only had Calkins satisfied all the customary requirements for the degree but the faculty further "voted to put on record that in their judgment the scholarly intelligence displayed by Miss Calkins was exceptionally high" (to President and Fellows of Harvard College, May 29, 1895, CWEPP). The response of the inflexible Harvard authorities was simply to acknowledge without comment the communication from the Philosophy Department regarding Calkins' successful completion of the requirements for the Ph.D. (June 10, 1895, CR).

At least one member of her committee went further in praising Calkins' performance and lamenting the withholding of the Ph.D. William James wrote to one of her Smith College classmates that

it was much the most brilliant examination for the Ph.D. that we have had at Harvard. It is a pity, in spite of this, that she still lacks the degree. Your downtrodden but unconquerable sex is fairly entitled to whatever glory and credit may accrue to it from Miss Calkins's prowess. (to Dear Madam, June 29, 1895, HNGP)

More informally, James is said to have exclaimed at the conclusion of Calkins' examination: "Now Santayana, go hang yourself" (Wolcott Calkins' Log, May 28, 1895, CFP). George Santayana, James' brilliant but arrogant young colleague, had until then enjoyed the reputation for the most outstanding performance on a Ph.D. examination in the Harvard Philosophy Department.

With her graduate study completed, Calkins returned to Wellesley in fall 1895 as associate professor of psychology. Here she continued to teach, to direct the laboratory, and to publish. In 1898 she was promoted to the rank of professor, the matter of her degree remaining unresolved.

Meantime, the Harvard Annex had been supplanted in 1894 by Radcliffe College, a chartered degree-granting institution. Radcliffe has been characterized by one educational historian as "perhaps the most exaggerated example of a college created solely on the basis of sex discrimination" (Schwager 1982:370). Schwager points out that "the college provided very little except the courses which otherwise were offered to men in Harvard College and instruction by the professors who otherwise taught Harvard men." What it accomplished for Harvard was a way of answering the incessant demand that women be given access to Harvard's educational opportunities while at the same time avoiding coeducation. Rather than allowing them to be physically integrated into Harvard,

Hugo Münsterberg (1863–1916). (Courtesy of the Harvard University Archives.)

women were offered a Harvard education, by Harvard professors but at Radcliffe College, and they were rewarded for their efforts with a Radcliffe degree.

Given the ongoing refusal of Harvard to grant the Ph.D. to several women who had completed their graduate studies there, the suggestion soon arose to award them a Radcliffe Ph.D. Münsterberg, who returned from Germany in 1897 to a permanent post at Harvard, wrote Calkins in November 1900 regarding the matter. Telling her that in Cambridge he and others had come to the conclusion that a woman's bid for fair treatment at Harvard was a lost cause, he counseled her to settle for the proposed Radcliffe degree with the reassurance that "everybody will know that [the] Radcliffe Ph.D. is given for the same work as the Harvard Ph.D. and it will have, therefore, exactly the same weight" (November 23, 1900, MWCP). And he confidently predicted that in a short time the Radcliffe Ph.D. would become "the leading American doctors degree for women."

Another year and a half elapsed before Radcliffe took the step of offering the Ph.D. In April 1902 the governing board of Radcliffe College voted to recommend Mary Calkins and three other women for the doctor's degree subject to the approval of the Harvard faculty, who gave it in May.[10] At the time these actions were being taken at home, Calkins was on sabbatical leave traveling in Europe. Münsterberg again urged her to accept the offer of a Radcliffe Ph.D., informing her with an air of finality: "The question is not anymore whether Cambridge ought to give the Radcliffe or the Harvard degree, but it has been settled that the Radcliffe Ph.D. will be the form of the Harvard degree for women" (May 20, 1902, HMP). Münsterberg reported that the plan to offer the Radcliffe Ph.D. had been accepted in a Harvard faculty meeting unanimously without a word spoken in favor of the Harvard Ph.D. In this meeting Münsterberg had told the faculty that Calkins remained dubious about accepting the Radcliffe degree. And President Eliot had responded with an attempt to convince his audience and Calkins that she could think of herself as a Radcliffe student even though she had never been enrolled there. His argument laid bare the gender discriminatory basis of the Radcliffe Ph.D. Münsterberg informed Calkins that Eliot had told the Harvard faculty: "You were no Radcliffe student, . . . simply because that which you were 'a woman studying in the Harvard Graduate school,' had at that time no special name while today that very thing is called Radcliffe student."

The official offer of the degree from the dean of Radcliffe, Agnes Irwin, reached Calkins in England. In her reply to Dean Irwin, Calkins enumerated her reasons for wishing she could accept the Radcliffe Ph.D. First, she told the dean that she sincerely admired the scholarship of the other women who were being recommended for the degree and would "be very glad to be classed with them" (May 30, 1902, RCA). Also she said she thought it highly probable that the Radcliffe degree would "be regarded, generally, as the practical equivalent of the Harvard degree." Finally, she wrote, "I should be glad to hold the Ph.D. degree for I occasionally find the lack of it an inconvenience; and now that the Radcliffe Ph.D. is offered, I doubt whether the Harvard degree will ever be open to women." However, Calkins continued, her conviction that "the best ideals of education would be better served if Radcliffe College refused to confer the doctor's degree" prevented her from taking "the easier course of accepting the degree."

Mary Calkins objected to the Radcliffe Ph.D. because it acquiesced to Harvard's stubborn refusal to recognize the accomplishments of women, like herself, who from the 1890s on studied in its graduate departments. Radcliffe never was in the business of graduate instruction. From its inception in 1894, the college, physically set apart from Harvard, offered only undergraduate instruction to women, courses taught within the confines of Radcliffe's walls by professors on the faculty at neighboring Harvard. Radcliffe itself offered no graduate courses or seminars, nor did it have laboratories for advanced work. Any woman who undertook *graduate* study did so not within Radcliffe but by going across to work at Harvard.[11]

Calkins viewed the decision to offer the Radcliffe Ph.D. to

women who completed requirements for the doctorate at Harvard as simply Harvard's device for continuing to deny recognition to women as legitimate students entitled to a Harvard degree. She was not willing to participate in the thinly veiled deception and chose to forgo the Ph.D. entirely.[12] Sixty years would pass before Harvard agreed to what Calkins doubted it would ever do once the Radcliffe Ph.D. was offered. In 1963 the subterfuge finally ended, and nearly seventy-five years after their entry into Harvard departments, women graduate students at last became eligible for the Harvard Ph.D.[13]

Although Calkins acknowledged that occasionally she found the lack of the Ph.D. inconvenient, it did not, in any apparent way, hinder her professional growth and scholarly achievement. She continued to teach at Wellesley until her retirement in 1929, all the while publishing prolifically in psychology and philosophy. Four books and well over a hundred papers are divided fairly evenly between the two fields. Her work in psychology is concentrated in the first half of her career; later philosophy became her dominant interest. Calkins' major contribution to psychology was a system of self-psychology that she presented, developed, and defended over a period of thirty years (Heidbreder 1972).

Elected president of two national professional societies—the American Psychological Association in 1905 and the American Philosophical Association in 1918—Calkins was the first woman to hold this office in each organization. Columbia University awarded her the honorary Doctor of Letters (Litt.D.) in 1909, and the following year Smith College bestowed on her the Doctor of Law (L.L.D.). Following her death in 1930, less than a year after she retired, a group of philosophers praised her as "an erudite scholar, a skillful teacher, and an incisive thinker" (Loewenberg and Roelofs 1930:323). They remembered her as "always patient and fair" in her criticism and "of incomparable courtesy" yet "steadfast in her positive convictions" presenting the truth as she saw it. In closing, they lauded their departed colleague as a woman who possessed a truly great capacity for friendship.[14]

Although Mary Calkins' life stands as a model of scholarly concentration and attainment, she did not regard the life of a scholar an easy one. An especially difficult task that the scholar faced, in Calkins' view, was the necessity to adjust the conflicting claims of demanding work and social responsibilities. She considered the adjustment to be particularly problematic for women, who had more exacting social and especially family obligations than men. This was true, Calkins maintained in a 1913 address entitled "The Place of Scholarship in Life" (MWCP), for the unmarried as well as the married woman. In an observation that reflected her own personal experience as well as the existing social norms, she remarked that it was an unmarried daughter rather than a son who was likely to become responsible for the care of aging parents. For the woman who chose to marry, the balancing act between career and family demands was even more difficult. Calkins mused over the married woman's plight without offering a solution: "How to be a scholar, though married is to tell the truth, one of the most specific problems of the scholarship of women."

In the next two chapters, the predicaments Mary Calkins described are exemplified in the lives of two early women psychologists. Chapter 2 takes up the issue of the obligations of a daughter to her family—the "family claim" as it was called—in the life of Milicent Shinn. Chapter 3 examines the marriage versus career dilemma as it was played out in the life of Ethel Puffer.

The Family Claim:
Ties That Bound Milicent Shinn

Milicent Shinn's biography in *Notable American Women* presents a puzzle. She began her career in San Francisco in the 1880s as editor of a literary magazine, a job she carried out successfully for over a decade. She went on to become the first woman to earn a Ph.D. from the University of California for a highly acclaimed study on the development of a child. At that point "around the turn of the century, while in her early forties, Dr. Shinn retired to the family ranch at Niles, and lived there quietly for the rest of her life" (Burnham 1971b:286). Her biographer concludes with an appraisal of her life: "Neither in literature nor in science had she sustained her early promise." Why did Shinn abruptly abandon professional activity in midlife? To understand this mystery it is necessary to know more of her story.[1]

Twenty-five years old in 1883 and just beginning her work as editor of the *Overland Monthly,* Milicent Shinn wrote an essay for the magazine entitled "Thirty Miles." It was a vividly detailed description of the sights that greeted her as she traveled from her rural home near Niles, California, to her editorial office in San Francisco at different times of the day and in different seasons of the year. She pictured for the reader fog banks and mists, cirrostratus and cumulus clouds, singing meadowlarks, wildflowers and orchards in bloom, groups of boys and girls traveling on the morning train from their homes in the country to attend school in Oakland, and the

Santa Cruz and Marin hills from her seat on the rear deck of the Oakland to San Francisco ferry (Shinn 1883).

"Thirty Miles" gave the pastoral, optimistic view of California life in the post–Civil War period. There was however another view, which was that "most of California in the decade of the 1870s seemed to be falling apart" (Starr 1973:132). Not only had the state experienced drought, crop failure, urban rioting, and depression, but there were also disturbing signs of social decay evidenced by San Francisco's high rates of alcoholism, juvenile delinquency, and street crime. Moreover, California had recently experienced a mass exodus of literary talent. In the 1860s Mark Twain and many other writers had congregated in San Francisco waiting out the Civil War, making it for a brief period the literary capital of the nation. In the following decade, as conditions in California worsened and there was peace once again in the East, these writers began to leave the state.

Shinn, a native Californian, thought the *Overland* could serve as a remedy for some of her state's current ills. She believed that it had the potential for replenishing the depleted stock of literary talent and that it could help in the moral and intellectual uplifting of the people of California, especially its youth. She prophesied that if the *Overland* were "built up into a powerful and wealthy magazine, it would supply the necessary inducement to young men of the right sort . . . to choose the literary life." And this, in Shinn's vision, would produce a new generation of Californians enobling the state by "its tendency to establish standards of simple, happy and sane living; to counteract social frivolity, business greed, extravagance, coarseness, class hostilities, and all the 'hastening ills' of the land where 'wealth accumulates and men decay' " ([Shinn] 1884:105).

The high ambitions for the monthly's future, which Shinn expressed in its editorial pages, were very different from her privately held sentiments. These she confided to Daniel Coit Gilman, president of Johns Hopkins University. She had first met Gilman when she entered the University of California in

Milicent W. Shinn (1858–1940). (Courtesy of the Bancroft Library, University of California, Berkeley.)

1874—only a year after it began admitting women and two years after it had moved to its Berkeley site. The hastily completed campus of what was then a remote provincial university has been described by one historian as consisting in the 1870s "of two four story buildings perched atop bare hills, one building of brick, the other of wood and both of monumental ugliness. When it rained, the unplanted campus became a sea of mud" (Starr 1973:147).

Shinn was one of a class of approximately eighty freshmen who arrived on the raw Berkeley campus in the last year of Gilman's brief presidency there before he left early in 1875 for Baltimore and the newly established Johns Hopkins. In 1879 she had a chance reunion with Gilman at a social science convention in the East, and he subsequently wrote advising her about opportunities for study at the newly formed Harvard Annex, which was headed by his cousin Arthur Gilman.[2] Thus began a cross-country correspondence between Shinn and Gilman that extended for many years and reveals a great deal about the young Californian.

Three years after their 1879 meeting, Shinn wrote that she had "cherished very longingly the idea of going" to study in Cambridge but admitted "the ties that keep me in California have been too tight." She added, "I did however, continue to hope to go there, until I found myself unexpectedly editor . . . of a magazine . . . much believed in by our best people as the possible germ of much civilization" (October 9, 1882, DCGP). She explained that she accepted the post "not as an advantageous position," but because the magazine "was at its last gasp—its last editor had left in despair, and it was going to die right there between the July and August numbers, if someone could not be found to step into the breach." And, she noted, as the job paid no salary "there was naturally not much competition." To make things worse, Shinn and the owner of the publication, who had been classmates at Berkeley, had inherited a "debt . . . scattered among pressing creditors." Telling Gilman it had been a life-and-death struggle to get each number out, she described their predicament: "We two do all the work, down to

carrying proof to the printing office, sweeping our office, past-
ing every wrapper, and mailing every copy." Shinn surmised
that it would be "disastrous to the feeble literary interests" of
her state if its sole literary magazine should fail. Yet she worried
over the fact that it had no capital behind it and could not pay
contributors. She then revealed to Gilman what prompted her
letter: "I am writing to beg you for your friendship to the
enterprise to give us an article."

Gilman would send an article, and he was to offer her continued support and encouragement in her work on the *Overland Monthly,* assuring her that her heroic efforts with the
magazine were indeed worthwhile. Shinn was frequently dis-
pirited, owing to the unexpected departure from California of
people whose advice and help she valued and the lack of capital that continually plagued the magazine. More than a year
after her request for an article, she wrote Gilman: "It is morti-
fying to me not to be able to make a better magazine of it"
(January 28, 1884, DCGP).

By August 1885 some capital had been raised and there was
hope of getting still more. Shinn was then considerably more
optimistic about the future of the *Overland,* noting in a letter to
Gilman: "We are by no means out of the woods, but I think I
may say we see our way through. . . . my brother and I have
taken the magazine solely into our hands, and it shows great
improvement and promise" (August 12, 1885, DCGP). Shinn's
optimism was not sustained, however. Five years later she
wrote to Gilman that her older brother Charles had married and
left the magazine. Moreover, she reported: "The magazine has
received some sharp set-backs, and . . . the difficulty of recovering them will be so great that we are considering giving
up the fight" (June 5, 1890, DCGP).

Shortly after this letter, Shinn became involved in a project
that would eventually lead her back to Berkeley as a graduate
student and establish her reputation in psychology. It came
about in an unplanned way, as had her editorship of the *Overland.* She resided throughout her life on the farm her family
had owned since her parents had come from the East to settle

in California in 1856. It was to this family homestead near Niles that her brother Charles brought his wife soon after their marriage and where, in fall 1890, their daughter Ruth was born. Being "the only child in a large household of grown people," Shinn recalled, the infant became "the object of a great deal of attention" (Shinn 1893–1899:5). Especially attentive to Ruth was her Aunt Milicent, who carefully observed and recorded in minute detail the child's physical growth and the development of her sensory abilities and reflexes—a documentation that continued for more than two years.

The scope and originality of the project, one of the earliest systematic accounts of a child's mental and physical growth, led to an invitation. It is not clear just how Shinn's work came to the attention of the conference organizers, but she was asked to deliver a paper describing her findings at the World's Columbian Exposition. This great fair, held in Chicago in the summer of 1893 to celebrate the 400th anniversary of America, featured a series of international conferences presenting advances in various areas of knowledge. One of the conferences was devoted to the topic of education, and it was here, among the papers on experimental psychology, that Milicent Shinn's contribution, "The First Two Years of the Child," appeared. Calling attention to the fact that little was known by teachers or psychologists about the mental abilities, interests, and ideas of very young children, Shinn pointed out that such knowledge was crucial in deciding how and when to instruct the child most intelligently. Careful studies of infant development were needed, she reasoned, because they could provide essential information to those entrusted with children's education (Shinn 1895a).

When Milicent Shinn began observing and recording the development of her niece, she was motivated purely by personal rather than scientific interest. Acknowledging that she had for many years sought an opportunity to watch how a helpless newborn baby evolved into a competent human being, she considered that this interest had quite likely come to her from her mother and grandmother who "had both been in somewhat notable degree observers of the development of babies' minds" (Shinn 1900:16). However, "unlike them," she observed, "I had the notebook habit from college and editorial days, and jotted things down as I watched, till quite unexpectedly I found myself in possession of a large mass of data." The notes she took were not originally intended for any scientific purpose, for she did not think herself competent at the time to make observations of any scientific worth:

I had no idea . . . of doing anything of serious value myself. I was absorbed in the baby, and simply took notes for my own pleasure and instruction, and was much astonished when I learned that no set of notes as copious and complete were known in this country. (Shinn quoted in Barus 1895:996)

Eventually becoming convinced by others that her work represented a significant contribution to the psychology of childhood, Shinn resigned as editor of the *Overland Monthly* in 1894 to begin graduate work as a candidate for the Ph.D. at Berkeley. She continued to observe Ruth's development through the child's seventh year and wrote a lengthy dissertation based on her findings. In addition, she took courses covering a range of subjects: child study, pedagogy, comparative physiology, sociology, anthropology, and psychology.

In December 1898 Milicent Shinn became the first woman and only the eleventh individual awarded a Ph.D. from the University of California. Her dissertation, "Notes on the Development of a Child," was published by the university in three installments, between 1893 and 1899. A popular version of her work, *The Biography of a Baby,* appeared in 1900 and was hailed by the reviewer, Christine Ladd-Franklin, as "a book which . . . no mother—and no psychologist—can afford to be without" (1901:142).

Wilhelm Preyer is sometimes credited with having published the first work of modern child psychology: *Die Seele des Kindes* (1882; translated as *The Mind of the Child* in 1888-89). His book was a detailed observational study of the development of Preyer's son. Shinn obtained a copy in 1891 just a few days after she began taking notes on her niece's development and acknowledged being instructed and guided by Preyer's work for some months into her own. Eventually, however, her study took its own direction: "As time went on, I departed more and more from the lines of Preyer's observations, and after the first year was little influenced by them" (Shinn 1900:17).

Preyer, after having read portions of Shinn's dissertation, was so favorably impressed with her work that he wrote to a colleague in America: "Miss Shinn's *Notes on the Development of the Child* ought to be translated for German mothers" (quoted in Chrisman 1900:192). While Preyer's work is usually cited as the preeminent study of its kind which set a standard for later similar efforts, Shinn is credited with the outstanding early American investigation of this type. And Preyer and Shinn are often included together as notable examples of early, systematic observational studies of children (e.g. Anderson 1933:4; Kessen, Haith, and Salapatek 1970:299–300).

Shinn's contribution to child development gained early and sustained recognition. In 1900 an educator familiar with Preyer's work wrote an enthusiastic review of her dissertation, declaring: "This is, perhaps, the fullest and best study of an individual child that has thus far been made" (Chrisman 1900:193). Moreover, the reviewer claimed that studies of the individual child such as Shinn's would "do more for the science of the child" than any other type of investigation he knew. He concluded by confidently predicting that as the field progressed "these *Notes* by Dr. Shinn will increase in value." In subsequent decades Shinn's work was hailed as a "masterpiece" (Mateer 1918) and as "a classic" that set the example for a long series of observational studies in America (Bradbury 1937). Today Milicent Shinn continues to be recognized in the most recent comprehensive handbook of child psychology as a pioneer in the field (Cairns 1984:61).

Yet Shinn's foray into psychology was brief, despite her ability and the acclaim her work received. As mentioned earlier, after completing her Ph.D., she abandoned scholarly and professional activity. This returns us to the question of why. We believe the answer lies in the societal forces at work that militated against the development of a professional identity even for highly educated women. Historian Joyce Antler has written of women's struggles to achieve professional identities at the end of the nineteenth and beginning of the twentieth centuries. She concludes that though some women—due to individual circumstances—were successful, nevertheless "women's search for a new identity remained largely unfulfilled" (Antler 1977:423).

Antler sees the reasons for this rooted for the most part in the social and political context in which these women were embedded. First there was the nexus of values and beliefs that assigned women to the sphere of domesticity and exerted "strong pressures against their identification as professional workers" (1977:408). Second, women's socialization to be daughters, wives, and mothers emphasized their responsibility to their families within the home and did not instill an expectation that they would pursue a vocation. Also the traditional feminine role that exalted the traits of nurturance, self-sacrifice, and submission was incompatible with the professional role that placed a premium on attributes such as individualism, dominance, and competitiveness (see Bledstein 1976 and Furumoto 1984). Finally, most women lacked the early exposure to the procedures, habits of thought, and conventions of the public sphere of business and the professions that many men acquired early in life. This could prove a significant disadvantage to women who aspired to make their way in the professional world.

In Milicent Shinn's case, her sense of responsibility to her family emerges as the overriding factor deterring her from forging a professional identity. Social reformer Jane Addams called this powerful family bond the "family claim." Addams coined the term at the turn of the century to characterize a source of conflict for the college-educated woman and contrasted the situation of middle-class sons and daughters in relation to it. She described the grown-up son as having "so long been considered a citizen with well-defined duties and a need of 'making his way in the world,' that the family claim is urged much less strenuously in his case" (Addams 1902:82). It was different, however, for the grown-up daughter, for whom "the years immediately following . . . graduation from college are too often filled with a restlessness and unhappiness which might be avoided. It is always difficult for the family to regard the daughter otherwise than as a family possession. . . . hard to believe that she has duties outside the family" (82–83).

Returning home after a significant period of intellectual training and relative social autonomy—an experience that prepared young men for a place in the public sphere—the woman college graduate was called upon to resume her role of family helper or daughter-at-home. The conflict between her desire for a life of her own and her parents' demands that she renounce ambitions outside the home sometimes led to a crisis in which the daughter typically experienced overwhelming feelings of futility and helplessness, depression, and occasionally even physical disability and illness. Often daughters managed to resolve the conflict by merging their own interests and goals with those of their families. In other cases, however, "the result for the women concerned could be severe and unremitting crisis" (Antler 1980:420).

The postgraduate crisis underscores a general truth in the experience of these women—the pivotal role played by the familial bond throughout their lives. Observing that family ties exerted a continuing influence on the choices college-educated women made about their lives, Antler maintains: "The family claim as Jane Addams termed it, aided in directing the paths on which women set forth, and in determining the manner in which alternate routes were perceived" (Antler 1980:420).

Milicent Shinn provides a dramatic example of the influence of the family claim on a woman's life course. The way the family bond was operating to shape Shinn's life can be glimpsed in a letter to Daniel Coit Gilman when she was twenty-one years old, at the beginning of the extended correspondence excerpted earlier in this chapter. Here she explicitly described how the responsibility she felt to her family stood in the way of realizing her aspiration to go east to study at the Harvard Annex. Telling Gilman how fascinated she was by his suggestion that she come to Cambridge to study at the Annex, she admitted: "It would cut half-a-dozen Gordian knots in my environment more thoroughly than anything else I can think of" (October 9, 1879, DCGP). What was holding her back, she confided, were her family obligations. The sole surviving daughter of four, she could not bring herself to urge her mother to let her "go for a year or several years, thousands of miles away." Furthermore, she told Gilman, her mother was not strong and her father was an elderly man of seventy. As for her two brothers, it was impossible for them, insisted Shinn, to fill the role of a daughter. Besides, she added, her older brother was away from home a great deal and living as they did in a neighborhood that lacked an adequate school, her younger brother was dependent upon her for his education. With an air of resignation Shinn concluded: "So you see, I am really needed at Niles, and Cambridge is out of the question."

The life of the scholar strongly appealed to Shinn; evidence for this emerges as early as her college years. Statistics compiled for the forty-three members of her graduating class at the University of California, the class of 1880, contain information for each individual on future occupation. Among the occupations given, which included the law, missionary work, mining, farming, and business, Shinn was unique in listing hers as "student." She wrote to Gilman on several occasions expressing interest in continuing her studies by taking courses at the Harvard Annex. Even the arduous years as editor of the *Overland Monthly,* which consumed her time and energy for more than a decade, did not completely extinguish her longing for the scholarly life. But her desire was continually tempered by a strong sense of family obligation.

Writing in 1890, for example, Shinn remarked that looking over the catalog of courses at newly established Clark University, where her cousin Edmund Sanford had been appointed to teach psychology, gave her "a homesick pang" and that she "sighed to be there" (June 5, 1890, DCGP). What she thought would be "the very best thing" for herself was "to be married to a scholar, and a helper in his pursuits . . . but failing that, the scholarly life itself is the most attractive." However she hastened to add that even if they would let her in and the magazine were off her hands, "I couldn't go. I couldn't leave my mother."

Only in 1894, when she was in her midthirties, was Shinn able to leave the magazine and enter the university at nearby Berkeley to study for the Ph.D. Even then, she did not see this major change as a first step toward launching a career. In explaining her reasons to one of her professors, she exhibited an impressive degree of self-confidence in the significance of her work. She was motivated, she told him, by loyalty to her alma mater, which she thought might profit from the widespread favorable recognition her study had received:

My main idea was not so much to get a Ph.D., as to give the university the benefit of the notice the observations on infancy that I had made seemed to be attracting. . . . I had been practically offered a Ph.D. at Stanford if I'd bring out the work there, and had been told that if it were practicable for me to fulfill the conditions of residence at Johns Hopkins or Clark, there w'd be no hesitation in recommending me for the degree there: so I thought if there was anything in it, my own University might as well have the benefit. (to G. H. Howison, September 8, 1898, GHHP)

Shinn began her work for the Ph.D. under the impression that the original research she had already done and some additional reading would be all that was needed for completion of the degree. Indeed, she contended that had she known otherwise, she would not have entered graduate school at all because of her financial and family circumstances. As she took up the advanced work, however, she found that she was held to more rigid requirements than she had anticipated. The result was that her study took much longer than she had planned. Compelling family needs and her own powerful response to them prompted her, in the fifth year of graduate work, to insist that she be allowed to take her degree that semester.

She wrote movingly of her reasons to one of her professors. The family was "heavily burdened with a mortgage" and for ten years her younger brother Joe had been standing it off, in the meantime "sacrificing his own advancement . . . entirely to the family interests" (to G. H. Howison, September 5, 1898, GHHP). During part of that period, Shinn had been tied up with the *Overland* and "restive under the knowledge that [she] ought to be helping him." Admitting that she had postponed this duty for too long a time and could not let the postponement "stretch out any farther," she insisted that she "must give [her] mind to the mortgage" and that she didn't "want the matter of a degree hanging over [her]." As she saw it, without question her family responsibilities took precedence over her personal wishes:

A young person chooses his line, and shapes his occupations toward it; but by the time you are 18 years out of college you are harnessed into your place in the working team, and can't shirk it: if you can get turned out of harness for an interval in pasture, so much the better; but you mustn't run away when the man comes with the halter.

Shinn did in fact finish that term, taking her final examination and receiving the Ph.D. in December 1898. She announced her achievement in a letter to Gilman and at the same time revealed a shift in focus from scholarly work to the imperative of the family claim. Expressing undiminished enthusiasm for scholarly pursuits, she admitted that henceforth they would have to be subordinated to family demands: "I have enjoyed the work immensely, and shall always keep it up; but as my family is circumstanced, it has to be in the intervals of other duties" (n.d., DCGP). Turning from her work in the psychology of childhood, which would be permanently put aside despite her hope to "keep it up," she redirected her energies to serving her family's needs. There was the mortgage to be paid, and she soon found herself centrally involved in caring for her invalid mother.

Seven years before, Shinn had already referred to her mother as "a delicate old lady" who was in poor health (to J. M. Schaeberle, December 27, 1891, LOA). A later letter reinforces this impression and illuminates the disturbing emotional impact her mother's illness had on her. There Shinn described their old family doctor as "a man I have been gladder to see now and then, in the middle of the night when I hung terrified over my mother, than anybody else on earth" (to E. S. Holden, May 14, 1895, LOA).

Shinn's life soon revolved exclusively around caring for her mother. The anxious quality of her attention and the depressed character of her commitment are conveyed in two letters to a friend in 1900. First explaining that her mother was not well enough to leave and that, consequently, Shinn was scarcely ever able to get away from home, she went on to describe the personal toll this was taking: "My time and strength go so much to the sickroom, the incessant wearing of anxiety, and the filling of all sorts of little stop-gap functions about house and ranch, that I can't really recommend myself to anyone as an interesting person to call on these days" (to W. W. Campbell, December 8, 1900, LOA).

Ten days later, in a similar letter, the theme of self-imposed isolation recurs. She explains, as if to herself, why she cannot accept an invitation to spend a few days away from Niles with friends: "Mother is liable to sudden and violent attacks of illness, not dangerous if I am right at hand to attend to them, but prostrating, and requiring great care" (to W. W. Campbell, December 18, 1900, LOA). Although Shinn admitted that her brother's wife Julia could see to her mother's needs, she did not feel that it was right to ask her to do this. She explained "she is daughter-in-law, and I daughter." The implication is clear: being a daughter carried with it in Shinn's mind a peculiar responsibility for looking after the welfare of one's mother, an obligation she could not shirk. She confessed that the "incessant and anxious strain of attention" she was being subjected to because of her mother's serious illness was extremely wearing. Yet she felt compelled to continue without respite: "This constitutes not so much a reason why I need a change and relaxation as a reason why I dare not take it. Eternal vigilance is the price of keeping her."

For more than a decade after she wrote these letters Milicent Shinn continued to serve as nurse and constant companion to her invalid mother. In 1910 she described yet another period of crisis, writing to a friend that her mother had been very ill and that she dared not make any appointments. Describing the progression from "a tiny cold,—nothing, I think, that any care could have avoided" to bronchitis and finally pneumonia, Shinn remarked that the doctors had held out little hope for her mother's recovery: "They said a delicate invalid of 84 could not throw off such a condition. But she did rally wonderfully, and has almost thrown it off" (to P. A. Hearst, September 30, 1910, PAHP).

We do not know just when Shinn's mother died. However, the numerous references to her mother's illnesses that figure so prominently in her correspondence through 1912 are missing by 1913. Although she was no longer preoccupied with her mother's care, she herself was now under doctor's orders to limit her activity because of a heart condition. Staying on at the Niles homestead, Shinn found another way to serve her family. Then in her midfifties, she took on the responsibility of tutoring her younger brother's four children, as she had once tutored that brother a quarter century earlier. Her reply to a request for information about an article she had written long before as editor of the *Overland Monthly* revealed the new direction her life had taken: "I have been hunting in the garret for the volume containing my old . . . article (so auntyfied has life become to me now that my books and papers are stacked up garret, that my den may be transformed into a school-room!)" (to W. W. Campbell, November 26, 1913, LOA).

Shinn would remain for the rest of her life on the family homestead, shaping her identity exclusively in terms of familial relationships. By the 1930s her four nieces and nephews were adults and she was in poor health. But with family still about her, she persevered in serving their needs in various ways. Her correspondence with Mary McHenry Keith, a friend for over fifty years since the time they were both students at the University of California, portrays Shinn's circumstances in the last few years of her life. Her older brother Charles had died in 1925, and his widow Julia had subsequently come to live with and look after her. Her younger brother Joe and his wife were neighbors, and she described them in a letter to Mary as "two old folks alone in the big house—their four youngsters all grown and gone" (May 13, 1937, KMcHPC).

Almost eighty, still not free from financial worries and suffering from lameness and other chronic ailments, Shinn nevertheless believed that her situation was satisfying in many ways. She wrote to her friend that she continued to find her time pretty well occupied with "business things and family things" (May 31, 1937, KMcHPC). For example, it was her responsibility to maintain a communication network with family beyond the boundaries of Niles, doing "all the corresponding with the aged and feeble members of the wide circle of the kindred." She confided that her brother wouldn't even be able to name all of these relatives. "There are at least 15 of them, some of whom write me weekly, some monthly, tell me when their children and grandchildren get married etc., etc."

Three years later in her last letter to Mary, written only weeks before Shinn's death in August 1940, she described her deteriorating health. But, most strikingly, the letter is filled with characteristic preoccupation with family. Telling her friend that she was "really aging in earnest," she elaborated on her condition by saying that she was "hardly able to sit up more than an hour a day" and that it was "hardly possible" for her to leave her room "even to go out in [her] own garden" (May 21, 1940, KMcHPC). She consoled herself with the fact that she had relatives about her—her sister-in-law Julia, her oldest nephew and his wife, and her brother Joe and his wife. Yet she lamented that although she was among family, "I am of little use to it now!"

Milicent Shinn's story powerfully dramatizes the impact of the family claim on the life course of nineteenth-century women. To recognize the strong and enduring ties that bound daughters, especially unmarried ones, to their families is to pierce the mystery raised at the beginning of this chapter. The answer to why Shinn left psychology and retired to Niles at midlife is, it seems, because her family needed her help there and she felt obligated to return. To paraphrase her own words, she was grateful for having been turned out of the family harness for an interval in pasture, but when duty called and it was time to get back into the halter, she knew she mustn't run away.

CHAPTER 3

The "Intolerable Choice": Ethel Puffer's Struggle with the Marriage versus Career Dilemma

Early women psychologists, and indeed all highly educated women at the time, found a common dilemma: whether to pursue the careers for which they had been trained or to marry and abandon professional activity. One woman stated the issue in these terms: "As human nature now stands and with woman's physical organization to consider . . . she ought to be taught that she cannot serve two masters, that if she chooses the higher path of learning and wants to do herself and her sex justice, she must forgo matrimony" (Helen Ridgely to C. Ladd-Franklin, October 15, 1897, CLF&FFP). Societal norms, husbands' expectations, and the belief systems of the women themselves militated against attempting to be both a professional and a wife.

The feminist and social critic Charlotte Perkins Gilman commented in 1906 on this lamentable necessity for women to choose between marriage and career, asking what it would be like if men confronted this decision: "Suppose every man had to choose between marrying the woman of his choice and instantly becoming a janitor for life, or remaining a bachelor and following the work he loved best" (Gilman 1907:496). Of course, she went on to point out, a man did not have to make such a decision, "he can be a husband and father and a member of society as well." On the other hand, "the woman must choose. She must renounce self-realization for . . . mother-hood." According to Gilman, this necessity to choose was leading a number of educated women to decline marriage in favor of a career. Moreover, she observed, many of those who remained unmarried were "contented and prosperous," pre-senting a challenge to the former attitude of "scornful pity which used to be given to the 'old maid' " (495).

The marriage rate of college-educated women in that era was low when compared to the marriage rate of women in the gen-eral population. Statistics drawn from surveys conducted in the early part of the twentieth century suggest that less than half of college women married whereas "in the population as a whole, over 90 percent married at some point in their lives, according to census figures from 1890 and 1910" (Solomon 1985:119). For some educated women, remaining single was a deliberate deci-sion, while for others the right suitor did not come along.

Milicent Shinn discussed the marriage rate of college women in *The Century* magazine in 1895. She drew attention to the fear that higher education might be unfitting women for do-mestic life: "Now that the question of the effect of college life on the health of women seems finally . . . settled, we are met by a new one, concerning its effect on their chances of mar-riage" (Shinn 1895b:946).

The statistics she had gathered and presented did indeed lead her to conclude that college women married at a much lower rate than other women and that those college women who did marry did so later than other women. Shinn pressed on to ask why they were less likely to marry, noting at the outset "that it is not because they crave a more exciting and public life; for the majority of them are schoolteachers" (947). Rather, she identified three other factors. The first was the widespread "employment of college women as teachers in girls schools." These cloistered environments provided precious little oppor-tunity for a college woman to meet a potential husband. As Shinn observed, there was "no station in life (save that of a nun) so inimical to marriage as that of resident teacher in a

Ethel Puffer Howes (1872–1950). (Courtesy of the Harvard University Archives.)

girls school" (948). The second cause was "the bent toward congenial marriage." Not only did the college woman set higher standards for an acceptable marriage partner, but she was also "under less pressure to accept what falls below her standard . . . because she can better support and occupy herself alone" (948). And finally, regretfully, Shinn admitted that she had "no doubt that the remaining cause of the low marriage rate is that many men dislike intellectual women."

Mirroring Shinn's statistics for marriage rates of college women, about half of the first generation of women psychologists did not marry. Most of these, as Shinn observed of college women in general, established careers in predominantly female academic environments. Within such settings they could find intellectual companionship as well as emotional support and fulfillment as part of a network of women who enjoyed deep and long-lasting friendships. Some developed a particularly close relationship with one other woman, a pattern "especially common among academic women at the end of the nineteenth century and the beginning of the twentieth century" (Faderman 1981:225).[1]

What happened to educated women who chose to marry? For some, the frustration of their professional aspirations generated incessant conflict. One of these in the first generation of psychologists was Ethel Dench Puffer (later Howes). Late in life, she reflected wistfully on "the golden age"—the days of her graduate school and early professional experience in Cambridge. Looking back on those years, Puffer said she was struck by how uncomplicated the intellectual lives of the graduate women, including herself, had been. They respected and found joy in scholarship, pursuing it without reservations. Furthermore, they had few doubts regarding "the worth of the scholar's life for women who chose it. The phrase, marriage versus career, had not been invented, to bedevil both thought and action" (Howes 1937:16).

Of course, the era that Puffer was remembering was one in which the choice between marriage and career did indeed pose a wrenching dilemma for many educated women. At the turn of the century, it had not yet become a significant issue in her own life, but soon it would. For in 1908 her professional activity was cut short by her marriage. Subsequently, what she called "the intolerable choice" became an increasingly absorbing subject for her. In fact, to reiterate her own words, it was a topic that later in her life would come "to bedevil both thought and action."

The eldest of four daughters, Ethel Dench Puffer was born in the eastern Massachusetts town of Framingham on October 10, 1872. On both sides of the family, several generations of her ancestors had been native New Englanders. Her father George had attended business school in Boston, where he worked as a railroad station master. Later he returned to his hometown of Framingham to become a useful and highly respected citizen, making a living as a station agent for the Boston and Albany railroad. Ethel Puffer's mother Ella also grew up in Framingham, the daughter of a successful cotton broker who spent his winters conducting business in New Orleans and summers in New England with his family. Two sons died in their youth, leaving Ella (born 1841) and her sister Caroline (born 1851) the only surviving children. The sisters were both provided with education beyond high school, unusual for young women in that era. Ella studied at a private school in Boston, and Caroline graduated from the normal school in Framingham. Both sisters, as well, had teaching careers. Ella taught in the local high school for seven years until her marriage in 1871, while Caroline, who remained unmarried, taught in a local elementary school. Ethel Puffer, then, grew up in a family where there was not only a precedent for higher education for women but also the example of women who had careers in the teaching profession.

After completing high school, Ethel Puffer herself traveled across the state of Massachusetts to attend Smith College, graduating in 1891 when she was not quite nineteen. The following year she took a teaching job at a high school in Keene, New Hampshire, and then returned to Smith for three years as an instructor in mathematics. At Smith, she became seriously

Ethel Puffer (left) and friend at Smith College, ca. 1890. (Courtesy of the Smith College Archives.)

interested in psychology, and in fall 1895 she set out for Germany, lured as so many other Americans were, by the opportunities to study at the universities there.

Being a woman meant, of course, that there were fewer of these opportunities available to Puffer than there were to young men. The review of a handbook of courses open to women in Britain, Europe, and Canada published at the time

Puffer was studying abroad made this explicit: "Those who have experienced the restrictions under which women study abroad will understand that a handbook of courses open to women in foreign universities is useful rather than agreeable reading" (Review of *Handbook of Courses Open to Women* 1896:411). England and Germany were singled out as countries particularly inhospitable to women. They were said to "give grudgingly what little they give, their motto being 'no rights and few privileges.' "

Puffer's initial experience in Germany did not contradict this pessimistic assessment. In lengthy letters home to her mother she cataloged her ordeals. After arriving in Berlin at the beginning of October, she wrote "They have all been frightening me with tales of the terrible difficulty of getting into the university here" (October 3, 1895, M-HP). She went on to explain that it was necessary for a woman student to secure permission by going to the home of each professor whose lectures she wished to attend. Furthermore, women were required to get permission from the rector, the official who headed the university, and from the government by applying to the minister of education.

More than two weeks later, on the day before the fall term was to begin, Puffer had not yet completed her arrangements: "There is still one man I haven't been able to catch. . . . They all live miles out in the suburbs and it is an afternoon's work to find them" (October 23, 1895, M-HP). That day in a pouring rain she had unsuccessfully attempted to find the rector: "I am really beginning tomorrow without permission either from the minister, the Rector, or the Professor! That sounds daring doesn't it?" Later, she confided that underlying her bravado she had been "much scared" by the prospect of going to the lectures "practically without permission" and knowing she would "be the only woman" in a lecture hall crowded with men (October 27, 1895, M-HP).

After her second day of attending lectures, she began a letter to her mother with the words: "This letter is not for public ears." There followed a confession that the stress she had been experiencing had begun to take its toll. That afternoon she had been seized with a "nervous headache." She was so violently ill that the family with whom she was boarding became frightened and sent for a doctor whose only advice to her was that she build herself up "with plenty of port wine and good food" (October 27, 1895, M-HP).

Eventually Puffer was able to work her way through the red tape necessary to get official permission to attend the university. And as the academic year progressed, she had some success in meeting people and in developing a satisfactory program of study. However, she became increasingly unhappy with life in Berlin. One source of irritation was the misunderstandings that arose because of differences between German and American norms for appropriate feminine behavior. Puffer described the distress of the American women students over gossip that the German professors were scandalized by the way the American women freely associated with the men, "let them walk home with them, etc. and that the University might very probably be closed to them after this" (December 20, 1895, M-HP). She also complained about her accommodations, saying that she was unable to sleep because there was so much noise in her lodgings and that the food was terrible. By the end of March she was wishing that she did not have to stay on through the summer to face "the horrid air and heat of Berlin" (March 29, 1896, M-HP).

In her classes she met a young Canadian who had taken his Ph.D. in psychology at Harvard while Hugo Münsterberg was there on a three-year appointment. Through him she was able to arrange an interview with Münsterberg, who was by then back teaching at the University of Freiburg. She was interested in aesthetics, one of Münsterberg's areas of specialization, and had attended a course of lectures on the topic at Berlin. Perhaps it was Puffer's knowledgeability and enthusiasm for the subject that prompted Münsterberg to extend an invitation to her at their first meeting. Much to her delight, he showed real interest in her, offering to direct her research and to let her work in his private laboratory. Moreover, Puffer's social life was very important to her, and Freiburg had great promise in this regard.

She knew of the Münsterbergs' reputation for hospitality from their Cambridge days, and Münsterberg himself assured her that his wife would help in making her stay in Freiburg a pleasant one. Understandably then, Puffer was elated about the prospect of leaving Berlin for Freiburg, and she wrote of her good fortune to her mother: "quiet, good air (Switzerland an hour away) and one of the three or four best men in Germany personally interested in me, and ready to further my aims socially and intellectually" (March 29, 1896, M-HP).

By early May, Puffer was settled at Freiburg and reported to her mother "work is now in full swing, and my hands to say nothing of my head are quite full" (May 4, 1896, M-HP). The university itself was not splendid; she described it as a "ramshackle tumble-down old place, formerly a Jesuit monastery, and the rooms are low and dark." While there were several other American students in her classes, she was the only woman and she told her mother at the beginning of her stay: "Of course I come in for a good deal of staring—but I am accustomed to that." A woman was also an oddity in a laboratory, something Puffer learned on the first morning she went to work with Münsterberg. The laboratory was located in his home, where Puffer was greeted at the door by a housemaid. When she asked for the professor, Puffer wrote her mother, she was told "in a deprecatory tone . . . 'the young lady probably does not wish to go to the laboratory.' "

Puffer spent the next year in Freiburg taking classes at the university and working in Münsterberg's laboratory—a year that was immensely successful for her both socially and academically. Adopted into the Münsterberg family, she thrived on the holidays, parties, cultural events, and outings that were an integral part of upper middle-class life in southern Germany. Carnival time, for example, was an especially festive season. "The three or four days before Ash Wednesday," Puffer told her mother, were "given up to all sorts of masking and mad frolics" in Catholic Freiburg (March 22, 1897, M-HP). She gave a glowing account of masked balls lasting late into the night where she "was besieged with [requests for] dances." Then there was a memorable party where "champagne flowed . . . like water" and several of Münsterberg's advanced students "were quite the event of the evening." They came to the costume party dressed as babies in long brightly colored gowns, making jokes and singing in unison a song they had composed in honor of their professor.

Not all of Puffer's time was taken up with such frivolity, however. She was also working diligently in Münsterberg's laboratory where he lavished his time and attention on her, individually supervising her research. Working on a problem in the psychology of beauty, she investigated the role played by symmetry in making a work of art aesthetically pleasing. For her study Münsterberg prepared "about a thousand pictures to test and measure for symmetry," and they spent mornings together working on her project. To allay any concerns her mother might have had about the propriety of this arrangement, Puffer wrote: "Don't be alarmed. Mrs. Münsterberg paints at the other end of the room and inquires when she does not understand our meaning" (November 11, 1896, M-HP).

Münsterberg considered Puffer's research so promising that he encouraged her to pursue it as a dissertation topic and to submit the work already completed in the competition for a graduate fellowship to be awarded by the Association of Collegiate Alumnae. In 1890 the ACA—a group of American women dedicated to promoting higher education for women— had begun granting two fellowships yearly for advanced work: one to be used for study in Europe, the other for study in America. Awarded solely on the basis of merit to women who showed promise of distinction in some line of original investigation, the fellowships were intended to encourage academically gifted young women to pursue postgraduate studies that would prepare them for scholarly careers.

Ethel Puffer, heeding Münsterberg's advice, applied for an ACA fellowship and won it. In the opinion of the selection committee: "Miss Puffer gave very unusual promise of a scholarly career" (Helmer n.d.:9). Included in their report was an excerpt from Münsterberg's letter of recommendation in which he stated that Puffer was the only American woman he had ever met whose abilities matched those of Mary Calkins. The award provided her with support for a year of work on her dissertation. Awarded the ACA's American fellowship for the academic year 1897–98, Puffer returned to New England, accompanying the Münsterberg family. Hugo Münsterberg had decided to return permanently to Harvard, where Puffer continued her dissertation work with him.

She completed the requirements for the Ph.D. by the end of the year and found herself in the same degree limbo as Mary Calkins, whose work had been finished three years earlier. Her situation was different from Calkins', however, in that by the time Puffer began studying at Harvard, Radcliffe College existed and Puffer was officially a Radcliffe student. She received only a certificate from the Philosophy Department documenting that she had successfully carried out work equivalent to that of candidates for the Harvard Ph.D. Copies were sent also to Radcliffe and the Harvard Corporation.

After waiting for three years, Puffer wrote to the dean of Radcliffe inquiring whether the college was willing to confer the Ph.D.: "I venture to make the first application, as the first candidate who holds such a certificate, Miss Calkins, not at the time a regular Radcliffe student" (to Miss Irwin, May 7, 1901, RCA). She explained that her reasons for wishing to set this precedent were that she had become convinced by a recent statement issued by President Eliot that Harvard would not change its policy toward granting degrees to women and that she feared the continued lack of doctoral degrees for women doing advanced work in Harvard departments would cripple graduate work for women there.

As a result of Puffer's overture, four women who had completed graduate work in Harvard departments over the previous several years were offered the Radcliffe Ph.D. in spring 1902. They were divided, however, among themselves about the wisdom of setting this precedent. Ethel Puffer was one of two women who accepted the degree; Mary Calkins was one of two who declined.

For a decade after her doctoral studies were completed, Puffer remained in the Boston area, dedicating herself to a career in psychology. During this time she held positions at Radcliffe, Wellesley, and Simmons colleges and published a book, *The Psychology of Beauty* (1905), based on her research in aesthetics. She was also being courted by a young graduate of the Massachusetts Institute of Technology who was a native of Keene, New Hampshire, where they had met when Puffer taught high school there. In August 1908, then in her midthirties, Ethel Puffer married Benjamin Howes, an event that brought her career in psychology to a halt.

Conspiring against her were not only academic hiring practices of an era in which married women were not viewed as appropriate candidates for teaching positions, but also the circumstances surrounding married life. She was hampered further by internalized norms that led her to believe it impossible to combine successfully the demands of professional life with those of motherhood. The inexorable negative impact that marriage had on Puffer's career was presaged by a rather sinister joke shared shortly before her wedding by a group of men who were her acquaintances at Harvard. In after-dinner conversation, the discussion turned to the "attractive young woman" doctorate who had recently become engaged to a young civil engineer, "a specialist in concrete construction [who] was to be married in the following month." Whereupon someone present quipped, it appeared that this woman scholar was "going to exchange the abstract for the concrete!" (Holt 1915:41–42).

The mere news of her engagement was sufficient to squelch Puffer's chances for an academic position in New York City where the couple planned to live. The president of Smith College, L. Clark Seelye, wrote concerning her candicacy for a position at Barnard College, "I fear the rumor which reached me concerning your engagement may have . . . affected the recommendation which I . . . sent, and that a candidate has already been selected to present to the trustees of Columbia" (April 29, 1908, M-HP).

Marriage changed the circumstances of Puffer's day-to-day existence beyond the loss of a professional position. She found herself having to cope with the traditional domestic responsibilities expected of middle-class wives. It was no easy matter, she wrote her mother in 1910, to manage a household and still find time for scholarship. Having just finished and put in the mail an important article, one she had promised to complete a year earlier, she was exhausted from the effort. She gave her husband credit for having taken on temporarily some of the domestic responsibilities: "Ben has helped me out somewhat— cooked everything one day" (Friday 1910, M-HP). Nevertheless, Puffer felt harried by the combined demands of household chores and scholarly work. "Of course there were things to attend to here always. Thank Heaven it is over and I can breathe." She confided to her mother that she was not yet an accomplished housewife. "Ben is happy as a lark making me over into a housekeeper of efficiency. Poor thing—I guess he gets discouraged enough!"

The task of satisfying her intellectual needs while fulfilling the demands of domesticity was proving difficult for Ethel Puffer, and it was soon to become even more problematic. In 1911 Ben Howes was temporarily assigned to a branch office of his firm and the couple moved to the isolated, rural community of Laurel, Mississippi. Early in their stay, Ethel's letters to her mother speak of days and weeks of hard work getting their living quarters habitable and becoming accustomed to what was for them an unfamiliar environment and people who had strange ways. Later letters suggest that the Howeses became caught up in a hectic round of social activities, some of which Ethel found a bore but endured because they were considered part of Ben's job. Writing to her mother in December 1912, she lamented, "It is awful the amount of invitations and social duties we have got into. We didn't really sit down yesterday, Sunday. Went to church, and to music in the afternoon, and all the rest of the time was cooking for me and housefixing for him" (December 4, 1912, M-HP).

Soon after they returned to New York from Mississippi,

Puffer's life took another turn that removed her still further from professional activities. When she was in her forties, she gave birth to two children: Ellen (1915) and Benjamin, Jr. (1917). In addition to her mothering responsibilities, Puffer took up activities in the public sphere, working for the suffrage movement and the war effort.

Ethel Puffer Howes struggled privately for many years with her dilemma as an educated, achievement-oriented woman whose decision to marry had cut her off from professional work. A glimpse into her life at that time comes from the reminiscences of a neighbor, Eva vB. Hansl, who wrote of the years when she and Puffer were raising their families and sharing their thoughts. Hansl recalled that she and her friend during that period of their lives had been "trying to resolve the conflicts of our desires to live in the larger world our education opened up to us and the smaller one of the home" (E. vB. Hansl to T. Weeks, June 3, 1952, EPP).

By the early 1920s, the demands on Ethel Puffer in both the private and public spheres were abating—World War I was over, the vote for women had been won, and her two children were approaching school age. It was then, as she was entering her fifties, that she began to publish her reflections on what she called "the persistent vicious alternative" confronting women: "marriage *or* career—full personal life versus the way of achievement" (Howes 1922a:444).

In 1922 Puffer published two articles in the *Atlantic Monthly* spelling out what she saw as an inherent contradiction in the notion that a woman could combine marriage and a career (Howes 1922a, 1922b). Her conclusion followed inexorably from the way she defined "career" and from her belief that for women marriage implied motherhood. Puffer claimed that for years the reality of the lives of educated married women had been generally ignored. In fact, she asserted, there was a conspiracy of silence operating to mislead talented young women about what they could expect of their future if they chose to marry.

Job discrimination was only one of several obstacles confronting the married professional woman. Even if every woman had the right to marry and go on with her job, Puffer maintained, she would still face several other stumbling blocks to success in a career. In describing these impediments, she was clearly drawing from her own struggles and experience. She observed that for thirty years the feminist Charlotte Perkins Gilman (whose comments on matrimony were considered earlier in this chapter) had "been inveighing against 'the wicked waste of housework' without making" so far as Puffer could see "a dent in the social mechanism." She scoffed at the absurdity of "references to labor saving devices as making the professional work of married women possible." She did not deny that the amount of labor—the time and energy—required in doing housework had been reduced, but asserted that this was not the crucial issue. Rather what was beyond the grasp of the young, married professional woman was "the possibility of mental concentration, of long-sustained intensive application, of freedom from irrelevant cares and interruptions, which every professional man knows is a dire necessity, if he is to touch success" (Howes 1922a:446).

This freedom, necessary for professional success, was made possible for the man by his wife, and Puffer enumerated "what every woman knows, the amount of subterranean ordering, protecting, fending off, which the ordinary career—for *men*—requires." In her view, this requirement for success—"the right to concentrate at need"—was something that "no young married woman, who is making a home with her husband, can now command" (446). Nor would she be able to command it until some mechanism was created to provide her with "basic household services—food, laundry, nursing, general housework," an eventuality that Puffer did not see in the offing.

Puffer cautioned that even if "the problem of the basic domestic function for women professional workers" could be solved so that "a modest household" could "operate without the personal entanglement of the feminine member" (447) there were still other hazards to be acknowledged. One of these concerned the likely incompatibility of the careers of husband and wife in a dual-career marriage. For as she pointed out, "If the feminine partner wants to set up a jungle laboratory, or a mountain observatory, we can imagine the author, though not the actor, as a husband for her" (448).

If in the future women were to hope to continue with their careers after marriage, Puffer advised that selecting a spouse would have to become more an affair of the head and less an affair of the heart, a pragmatic decision based upon how well the careers of the prospective partners meshed. A lesson could be learned, she counseled, from the "hundreds and thousands of talented women, who have married for love . . . [and] have found the world of work lost to them" (449).

But the pitfalls of household entanglement and of career incompatibility paled before what Puffer described as "the supreme self contradiction" in the life of the married woman who wanted a career. Granting that "there have been happy marriages without children, as there have been full lives without marriage" (449), she insisted, nevertheless, that the motherhood issue had to be addressed since it was an integral part of the lives of most married women. Being a mother and having a career were inherently contradictory in Puffer's view, for a career meant competition with men who accepted the fact that they could not expect to achieve "without the most intense and most ruthless concentration" (449). And she simply did not believe that women who were mothers were capable of this. Motherhood, she maintained, not only produced a kind of psychological disability for concentrated mental effort but also imposed on women a set of ironclad responsibilities to one's children that precluded professional commitment.

She felt certain of the fact that the experience of motherhood altered a woman's values so that "self absorption in a task apart" became "less possible to her" (450). As a consequence of motherhood, the professional woman would face in her job "innumerable . . . mental conflicts between preoccupation with her children and duty to her performance." And the way Puffer saw it, "whether the children suffer or not, the quality of her work must suffer" (450). Even if it were possible for the mother to "summon her whole energy of mind to outside work," Puffer reasoned, "the child whose mother is not *on call* is bound to lose" (451). The necessity that the mother be continually available for the welfare of the child meant to Puffer that mothers, unlike fathers, were never free to pursue their professional work unmindful of their children.

Educated women, then, found themselves caught in an irreconcilable dilemma, Puffer argued. She saw them: "forced by a normal principle of growth to seek to use fully the abilities which their education has set free, [while] a natural and original principle in turn saps their effort at its spring. Women are both inevitably impelled to, and interdicted from, marriage, children, and careers" (Howes 1922a:452). As long as the culture defined careers as all-consuming, and as long as women were assigned all the responsibility for the nurturing of children, there could be no solution to the dilemma.

Puffer laid out her answer to this problem in her second *Atlantic Monthly* article "Continuity for Women." She emphatically rejected the suggestion that the talents of educated women could find adequate expression within the home, asking, "Would an entomologist find the full expression of his science in keeping his household free from insect pests? Would he continue to be an entomologist at all if that were the extent of his activity?" (Howes 1922b:733). Having dismissed the "home use theory" of educated women's abilities, Puffer proposed an alternative. She challenged women to forgo careers in traditional sense in favor of professional work that could be accomplished on a flexible timetable as their primary responsibility of mothering permitted. Acknowledging both "the well-trained woman's need of carrying on after marriage [and] the mother's inability for an output of a certain quantity, deliverable without interruption," Puffer insisted that the educated woman who became a mother would not be "falling short of her professional ideals in contracting the scope or modifying the type of her work" (736).

How to enable "the trained woman, who finds her profes-

sional activities coming to a full stop in marriage and motherhood" to achieve continuity became a project of central
importance in Ethel Puffer's life through the decade of the
twenties (Howes 1923:32). Her *Atlantic Monthly* articles
stirred interest among influential people, leading Puffer to
formulate a proposal for a foundation that would develop
methods "allowing the wife and mother completely to fulfill
her home responsibilities, while continuing some systematic
work for which she has been trained" (quoted in Mohraz
n.d.:7).

A grant from the Laura Spelman Rockefeller Fund in 1925
financed the Institute for the Coordination of Women's Interests at Smith College with Puffer as director. During the
three-year grant period, while her two children were still in
elementary school, Puffer commuted from her home near
New York City to western Massachusetts. A newspaper article on the institute that appeared several months after it started
highlighted the life-style of its director:

Mrs. Howes leaves for Northampton either Sunday night or Mon-
day morning. Before leaving she plans the children's afternoons for
the next three days, decides what they shall wear to school, what
they shall eat for dinner—the innumerable details of "just living"
which every mother knows exceedingly well. She is in Northampton
until Wednesday night, busy at the college all day with institute
work, correspondence, lectures. She has a room in the co-operative
kindergarten house. Thursday morning she is back in Scarsdale,
gathering up the innumerable threads of family life. (*Boston Herald,*
April 10, 1927)

Puffer was candid about the fact that according to her standards this was "by no means an excellent arrangement" from
"the family point of view." It meant that much of the time she
had to be away from home and was therefore unable to re-
spond to her children's needs for comfort, aid, and companionship whenever they arose. However, in spite of her conflict
over the "mother absence" which her role as director of the
institute dictated, she persisted in her work.

Letters to her aunt, written while she was commuting by train, reveal the hectic pace of Puffer's life. Caught between the demands of her job and her domestic and family responsibilities, she could find little time for herself and was at times pushed to the brink of exhaustion. In addition to her work at Northampton she was also attending out-of-town meetings, trying to raise additional funding for the institute, and giving lectures on the work going on there. Describing a lecture tour in the spring of 1926 that included Boston, Providence, and New York City, she told her aunt: "I have been making speeches *ad nauseam*. Accepted too many invitations early in the year, now coming home to roost! . . . all this speaking work I quite enjoy, but the travelling is killing" (April 26, 1926, M-HP).

In the three-year grant period, aided by the institute staff, Puffer carried out an impressive array of projects. One of these was a survey of five hundred Smith alumnae identified by the institute as successfully coordinating family and work responsibilities. Another project included developing a cooperative nursery school and a food service that delivered hot meals to families. These demonstration programs were designed to reduce women's domestic responsibilities thus freeing them for other work. The institute also conducted research to identify occupations that would meet women's needs for flexible schedules, singling out among others, free-lance journalism and domestic and landscape architecture.

Yet, despite the productivity of the institute and the fact that it appeared to be addressing a matter of real concern to many women, its funding was not renewed; as the 1920s drew to a close, it was phased out of existence. The Rockefeller Fund did not renew its grant. Presumably, this occurred because, in the foundation's view, the institute had devoted its efforts too much to applied research and not enough to developing a theoretical framework for coordinating women's interests. Also, the Rockefeller Fund had hoped that the institute would be integrated into Smith College and its aims reflected in the curriculum. This did not happen. Many faculty opposed the undertaking, believing that it represented a deviation from the liberal arts ideal toward vocationalism or even home economics.[2] After her heroic efforts to make a success of the project, Puffer felt misunderstood and discouraged by the withdrawal of the Rockefeller support and the resistance of the Smith faculty. A book she was to write as director on the institute's philosophy and conclusions did not appear. In her late fifties when the project was terminated, Puffer turned her attention to other interests, ending her professional involvement with the issue of coordinating educated women's needs for intellectual as well as personal fulfillment.

In her *Atlantic Monthly* articles of 1922, when she expressed the inherent contradiction for women in combining marriage and motherhood with careers, Puffer's way of resolving the dilemma was to redefine careers for women rather than to suggest redefining marriage and motherhood. This way of thinking, as historian Judy Jolley Mohraz points out, was prevalent among professional women in the late nineteenth and early twentieth century:

They could reject prevailing notions of women's proper activities and stride into the male dominated professional arena. They could not, however, alter or reject their ideas about women's domestic duties; neither could they advocate the restructuring of the home, marriage, and childrearing that would enable them to pursue their careers after marriage. (Mohraz n.d.:14)

In her last public utterance on the marriage versus career issue in 1929, Puffer did seem to be calling for just that, a redefinition of women's traditional role to eliminate forever what she referred to as "the intolerable choice" (Howes 1929, 6). Changed perhaps as a result of her experience with the institute, she no longer believed that "special devices" and "personal adjustments" would enable women to "participate in both professional and family life." Instead, she envisioned the necessity of "transforming the whole social setting and the inner attitudes of men and women to accept the twofold need of women as fundamental."

CHAPTER 4

Meritocracy in Science:
Margaret Floy Washburn's Use of the Myth

It is widely believed that science, as a social institution, generally operates as a genuine meritocracy, a system whereby deserving people are recognized and rewarded on the basis of their professional achievements. The criteria used to assign merit in science are ability and research performance. A successful scientist's ability includes a well-trained intelligence and knowing how to use one's training and experience. Such ability is necessary to produce research and scholarly works of sufficient quantity and quality to gain a reputation and the respect of one's peers and the honors they can confer. If science indeed functions as a meritocracy, then such particulars as an individual's age, race, gender, social class, and ethnic membership should not matter in the distribution of the rewards that signify success.[1]

Here we explore the issue of meritocracy in psychology by examining the career of the most accomplished of the women psychologists. Of all the women in the first generation, Margaret Floy Washburn best exemplifies a thoroughly professional psychologist. She began advanced study in psychology immediately after graduating from college and followed a virtually unbroken academic career pattern. She conducted research, wrote a major textbook, and devised an impressive theory. She participated in psychology's organizational activities on regional, national, and international levels. And for her contributions to the field, she received unusual recognition from her peers.

Several factors account for Washburn's success in gaining eminence among the early American psychologists: family background and support, educational and employment choices, and personal qualities including high motivation, a strong, positive self-image, and an exceptional ability to fraternize with colleagues. But gender was also a salient factor in Washburn's career, for being a woman meant that in spite of her prodigious ability and accomplishments, she was limited in certain ways: she was denied important opportunities for career advancement that were available to the men who were her peers. Washburn's response to the constraints she experienced as a woman was to proceed as if gender made no difference, as if the merit system applied fairly to women as well as men. In her case, the strategy worked remarkably well.[2]

Margaret Floy Washburn was the only child of Francis Washburn and Elizabeth Floy Davis. All of her ancestors were settled in America before 1720, with the exception of Michael Floy, her mother's maternal grandfather. He came from Devonshire, England, around 1800 and operated a prosperous business in New York City, with a florist shop in Bowery Village and a nursery located on a tract of land in Harlem on upper Manhattan Island. The Floy family traditions were quite influential in Washburn's development. Significant clues to her attitudes and values are found in the diary kept by her great-uncle, Michael Floy, Jr., which was published over a hundred years later in 1941. The printed edition includes an introduction, annotations, and postscript by Washburn, who was preparing the diary for publication before her death. The editor who completed the work noted in his preface the

curious similarity of mind between her and her ancestor. . . . Common to both were the catholicity of taste, the love of music, the love of animals that was devoid of sentimentality, the warm concern for the needy and unfortunate, the modesty, the free and inquisitive mind that was doggedly honest with itself and, despite its many facets and interests, had a vein of iron rigidity in it. (Brooks 1941: v)

Margaret Floy Washburn (1871–1939). (Courtesy of Archives of the History of American Psychology, University of Akron.)

In 1837 the Floys moved to a residence built on the Harlem property, where homes were also built for the families of the two married daughters. One of these married James Davis, a prosperous merchant. The Davises had two daughters, Elizabeth (Margaret Washburn's mother) and Caroline. Caroline, five years the younger, was sent to Vassar College at its opening, graduated in 1869, and received the M.D. degree from Zürich in the 1870s. Elizabeth married Francis Washburn. His father was both a pharmacist and a minister to Methodist parishes in the New York counties of Westchester and Orange, and his older sister was principal of a New York City public school before her marriage. Washburn, then, came from a family that had on both sides exceptionally able women who served as role models and set a standard of academic accomplishment.[3]

Margaret Washburn was born on July 25, 1871, in the large frame house that had been built for her grandparents in the Floy family compound. Her father was then in business. She later described him as a "constant reader" with a "considerable literary gift but like his father limited through lack of educational discipline." According to her, he also had a "violent temper and much fluctuation of mood." Her mother had completed high school in New York City and was in her daughter's words: "The most perfectly balanced nature I have ever known. Her natural strength and sweetness of character were only increased by the difficulty of living with my father. She had a fine mind and read widely; she had musical talent." Interest and ability in music were strong family traits on both sides. Music was also important in Washburn's personal and professional life. As a psychologist she devoted considerable attention to experimental study of the emotional aspects of music, winning in 1921 a national prize presented by the Edison Phonograph Company for the best research on the effects of music.

When Washburn was growing up in Harlem, it was a residential suburb, "cut off from the rest of town by the vacant spaces and the shanties of the Seventies, Eighties and Nineties" (Footner 1937:282). It was like a separate city, distinct in its characteristics, with its own elegant streets and a great shopping thoroughfare. She spent her childhood in this quietly dignified neighborhood, removed from the turmoil brewing in the crowded city to the south with its influx of immigrants, burgeoning urban problems, and political intrigues. Though her family was comfortably middle-class, their strong Methodist affiliation and their geographical separation from the heart of the city also isolated her from certain concerns of the "society people," such as their emphasis on status manifested in fine eating, fashionable clothing, and money. She nevertheless acquired some values of the old New York gentility: insistence on "form" and "taste" and "beautiful behavior"; rituals for ignoring the unpleasant; fascination with travel, horticulture, and fiction; verbal niceties; and the importance, for women, of possessing good looks, health, grace, and cleverness.[4]

Her family's money, coming from the Floys, assured Washburn of a comfortable home and certain amenities. When she was twelve years old, she and her parents took a trip down the Mississippi River from St. Louis to New Orleans. Two years later they traveled to Europe and the British Isles. Her first formal education was at a private school run by the Misses Smuller in the home next to hers, where she studied arithmetic, French and German, and music. Following her parents' example, she became a voracious reader. As an only child, she cherished her privacy, and the self-reliance she developed stood her in good stead later in life, when she was often alone. Thus she did not experience solitude as deprivation, remarking often "never less alone than when alone" (Macurdy 1940:3).

Francis Washburn entered the Episcopal ministry when his daughter was about eight years old, and thereafter he served as pastor to congregations in several rural communities in the Hudson Valley. As the family moved about to accommodate his work, she attended both private and public schools, graduating from Ulster Academy in Kingston, New York, in 1886 at the age of fifteen. She then entered Vassar College at nearby Poughkeepsie. Because she lacked some entrance requirements, her first year at Vassar was spent as a preparatory student and therefore her time there was extended to five years. During those years she pursued a wide range of intellectual interests, recounted in detail in her autobiography. It was an exciting period for her, filled with stimulation and "mental expansion" (Washburn 1932).

Washburn studied psychology and ethics in her senior year, as was common in the college curriculum of the day. The course was taught by Vassar's president, who "wished to preserve [the] religious conviction" of his students by "saving" them from both materialism and pantheistic idealism (Washburn 1932:338).[5] His pleading came too late for her, however. She had already dropped "orthodox religious ideas," having been strongly influenced by the religious radicalism of an older student (337). She was also a college editor in her senior year and in that capacity reported on lectures delivered at Vassar by President J. G. Schurman of Cornell University, never suspecting that she would in a few years become one of his students. When she wrote of her college days and her growing love of poetry and philosophy forty years later, she recalled another influence: "Matthew Arnold, with his matchless combination of classic beauty, clear thinking, and deep feeling became my favorite; I wrote my Commencement oration on 'The Ethics of Matthew Arnold's Poetry,' tracing the Stoic elements in it" (Washburn 1932:337). Arnold's writings continued to be a source of pleasure for her. The four elements she identified in him—beauty, clear thinking, deep feeling, and stoicism—also characterized Washburn's personal life and career. But for her they were demonstrated in the context of experimental psychology rather than literature.

"At the end of my senior year," she wrote in her autobiography, "I had two dominant intellectual interests, science and philosophy. They seemed to be combined in what I heard of the wonderful new science of experimental psychology" (Washburn 1932:338). So Washburn decided to study the subject with James McKeen Cattell at Columbia University immediately after graduation from Vassar. Her parents supported her plan and took a house in the city for the year so that she might have a proper residence. Columbia's policy of excluding women, however, meant that she could not be admitted to classes until the trustees met in December to consider her special case. She spent the fall semester fruitfully, nevertheless, reading and translating from German an article on scientific methods by Wilhelm Wundt, at the suggestion of the dean of the Philosophy Department.

Washburn was finally permitted to attend Cattell's classes—but only as an auditor since Columbia refused to accept her as a regular graduate student. Nevertheless, she enjoyed equal status in Cattell's eyes and such encouragement from him that she later wrote: "I feel an affectionate gratitude to him, as my first teacher, which in these later years I have courage to express; in earlier times I stood too much in awe of him" (Washburn 1932:339). Cattell, however, wisely recognized her need for more than could be provided by Barnard, the women's college associated with Columbia, and advised her to apply for a graduate scholarship at Cornell University, where she might be admitted as a degree candidate.

At Cornell Washburn was awarded the prestigious Susan Lynn Sage Fellowship in Philosophy and Ethics. E. B. Titchener, who had recently trained at Leipzig under Wundt and was the only experimental psychologist on the Cornell faculty, was the adviser for her experimental work, but her special friends were the philosophy professors. She completed her doctoral study in two years and was granted the Ph.D. in June 1894, becoming the first woman ever to receive the doctorate in psychology. Titchener took the initiative of sending her thesis, which explored the influence of visual imagery on judgments of tactual distance and direction, to Wundt for publication in his journal *Philosophische Studien*. This was a clear indication of Washburn's early promise as well as a singular honor for an American student, as Wundt rarely published work by anyone other than his own students. A few years later, Washburn was the English translator of the second volume of Wundt's *Ethics*.

The year she received her degree, Washburn was elected to

membership in the newly formed American Psychological Association, where she joined two other women, Christine Ladd-Franklin and Mary Calkins. During the next forty years, Washburn actively participated in the affairs of the association and was widely recognized for her contributions. The development of her theoretical stance and her experimental interests may be traced through the papers she delivered at the annual meetings. More significant for her professional development, however, was her involvement in important policy-making positions. In 1912-1914 she was a member of the influential council of the association, one of only three women to hold that position during the first forty years of the APA's existence. Thereafter she served on several important committees, often as chair. It was quite unusual for a woman to fill such leadership roles. Among the first generation of women only Washburn and Mary Calkins did so.

Washburn became president of the APA in 1921. By then she had become firmly established as a member of psychology's inner circle. She had gained respect for her experimental work early in her career, had maintained contacts with the influential men at both Columbia and Cornell, and had extended her professional network to establish relationships with colleagues at other centers of academic psychology. She had increased her visibility and widened her sphere of influence through frequent publishing, editing several scholarly journals, traveling to meetings, and simply by doing what she called "hack work"—all necessary for building acceptance, respect, and a strong reputation. She was clearly the most prominent woman in academic psychology.

These achievements could not have been predicted at the time Washburn left Cornell in 1894. Indeed, during the next several years her career direction was unclear. The year before completing her doctorate, she had been offered a position at a women's college in Cleveland but decided, against the advice of President Schurman, to remain at Cornell to finish the degree. Unsure about what she might do when she completed her training, she even considered teaching at a finishing school

Group of former American Psychological Association Presidents, 1930s. Pictured are (front row, left to right) Joseph Jastrow, Carl Seashore, H. C. Warren, Margaret Washburn, Robert S. Woodworth, (back row) Knight Dunlap, Raymond Dodge, Harry L. Hollingworth, and Lewis M. Terman. (Courtesy of Archives of the History of American Psychology, University of Akron.)

in New York City. Meanwhile, however, she received an offer to join the faculty of Wells College, a women's college located about twenty-five miles from Cornell. She accepted the offer and went to teach philosophy and psychology there while maintaining relationships with the Cornell faculty through frequent visits to Ithaca. When she became ill one

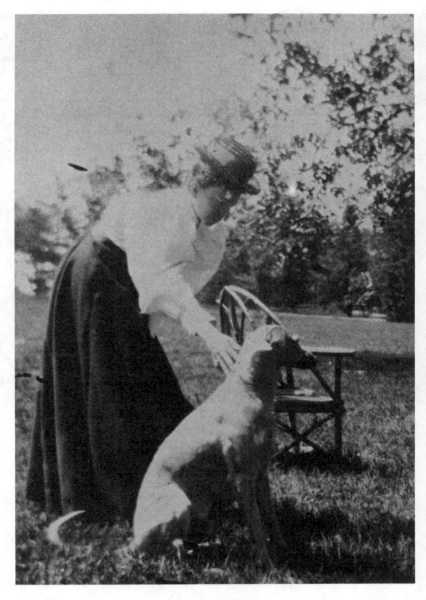

Margaret Floy Washburn at Wells College, 1890s. Deeply fond of animals, her most influential work was The Animal Mind *(1908). (Courtesy of the Wells College Library.)*

summer and was unable to return to work at Wells until December, her Cornell friends were unusually supportive. Without her knowledge, two Cornell philosophy professors took charge of her classes, traveling twice a week from Ithaca to cover for her. After several satisfying years at Wells, having attained the highest salary possible for a woman ($700 a year and "home," which was a room in the student residence hall, whereas the men were paid $1500), she became restless and was ready for a change.[6]

In 1900 Washburn accepted an offer to become warden of Sage College, the dormitory for women at Cornell, a position comparable to dean of women at other coeducational institutions. There she had the "enormous salary" of $1500 as well as free living quarters. In addition to her administrative duties, she was appointed lecturer in psychology during her second year and gave two courses, each of which foreshadowed areas that would become increasingly important in her intellectual development—social psychology and animal psychology. She found, however, that having to supervise the personal and social lives of the young women under her care did not suit her reserved temperament and so welcomed an offer of an assistant professorship at the University of Cincinnati.

Washburn's personality and the offer combined to enable her to escape the entrapment in the student affairs branch of academia that became the destiny of some talented women scientists.[7] In 1902–3 she was the only woman faculty member at Cincinnati, a municipal university established in 1870 which had an 80 percent female student body by 1900 (Solomon 1985). In addition to her isolation among the faculty, there were several other drawbacks for her there, including an unwelcome separation from her parents. Furthermore, as she commented, "It is hard for a deeply rooted Easterner to be transplanted" (Washburn 1932:345).

At some time during these years Washburn confronted the marriage versus career dilemma and decided on psychology as a career over marriage to a colleague who was a philosophy professor at Cornell. Though the necessity to choose between marriage and career was a painful source of conflict for many women, Washburn was apparently comfortable with her decision and seems not to have felt unfulfilled without marriage and children.

In 1903 Washburn was delighted to be invited to Vassar as associate professor of philosophy. Returning to her alma mater, she enjoyed a position of considerable importance in a congenial setting and also was able to visit every Sunday with her parents, who then lived in a nearby town. From that supportive base, she pursued a long and fruitful career that included not only the organizational activities mentioned earlier but also teaching, directing student research, participating in college affairs, and developing her theory of consciousness. These activities together with travel and personal pursuits in music, drama, history, and literature gave her a full and satisfying life for more than three decades. In March 1937 Margaret Washburn suffered an incapacitating cerebral hemorrhage; she died in Poughkeepsie on October 29, 1939.[8]

Washburn's accomplishments and her connections with powerful and sympathetic men brought her unusual distinction as a psychologist. Her highest achievement was election to the National Academy of Sciences in 1931, when she became the second woman admitted to the most eminent scientific society in the United States.[9] Margaret Rossiter (1982:71–72 and 110–11) has described the politics involved in getting women elected to the academy. It is clear that Washburn's election was the result of widespread support among psychology's influential men who acted like "big brothers" on her behalf. The recognition she received suggests that the scientific community was acting fairly in her case, assigning merit on the basis of her work rather than discriminating against her because of gender. While peer support was successful in winning her admission to the National Academy, there were nevertheless certain other limitations imposed by her gender: Washburn was excluded from membership in the elite group of psychologists known as the Experimentalists, and she was denied an academic post at a major research university, the position from which ambitious men successfully pursued their careers in psychology.

Given Washburn's reputation, had she been a man, she would certainly have been offered such an appointment. Given her interests, she would no doubt have welcomed such an offer. But at that time women were not considered for faculty posts in the psychology or philosophy departments at any major Eastern university. The exclusion of women from these positions apparently was not a matter of considering and then rejecting them; rather the idea of hiring women as regular faculty was simply not entertained.[10] Washburn did teach in the Columbia Summer School for five years (while the regular faculty took vacations) and "admired the chances of fortune that had raised me so high" that she could occupy "Dr. Cattell's office" during that time (Washburn 1932:349).

So it was from Vassar, a women's college with no graduate program in psychology, that Washburn had to proceed in advancing her career. Her successes brought considerable acclaim to Vassar—she "put Vassar on the psychological map." The unusual character of her accomplishments becomes clear by examining the institutional affiliations of people who served on important committees and editorial boards during the first several decades of the twentieth century. Here the research universities are well represented as are the prestigious men's colleges, and certain of the land-grant state universities. There often appears in these lists, however, a single women's college—Vassar—an anomaly in such company. In these instances, it was the person, Washburn, who brought distinction to the school rather than the other way around.

At Vassar, Washburn was subject to the limitations experienced by all faculty at the women's colleges: heavy teaching loads, inadequate resources for research, expectations of considerable involvement in student affairs, and lack of stimulating collaboration with colleagues in one's own specialty area and advanced students.[11] In addition, there was a strong ethos of faculty loyalty to the college community as a primary attachment, which drew energy and attention away from involvement in the off-campus activities that might further a professional career in a discipline. Washburn managed to surmount these obstacles with remarkable success.

She was clearly more attracted to scientific research than to teaching, and by combining her interest in research with her required teaching, she managed to produce a significant series of research reports. Under the title, "Minor Studies from the Psychological Laboratory at Vassar College," more than seventy articles were published in the *American Journal of Psychology* over a 33-year span. For these she had students in a senior seminar conduct studies that she designed and then prepared for publication under joint authorship with the student as collaborator. In this way she was able to explore her own ideas, maintain a presence in experimental psychology by making substantive contributions, and at the same time meet some of her teaching responsibilities. Students tended to view her as an excellent teacher—authoritative, clear, organized, brilliant in classroom lectures—but aloof and distant in interpersonal relations (Goodman 1980b). Though she did participate in campus events involving students, as well as in faculty affairs, she did not get caught up in her students' personal lives, perhaps because of having learned earlier at Wells and Cornell that, for her, such activities were often unwelcome distractions. She avoided social isolation, however, through rich friendships with certain Vassar faculty, both men and women, and by determined efforts to maintain strong relationships with others in her field through travel, correspondence, and continued involvement in professional affairs.

Washburn was one of an emerging breed of college professors, those who saw themselves as "professionals" in terms of their scholarship and held allegiance to their academic disciplines rather than to home institutions. While she retained a devotion to Vassar College, her participation in the activities of professional psychology on a broad scale was equally important to her—perhaps even more so. Insofar as her preferred vocation was science, she differed from other early academic women psychologists, who continued to maintain a primary commitment to teaching and the life of the institution where they were employed.[12]

Henry Noble MacCracken, president of Vassar College for much of Washburn's tenure there, classified the Vassar faculty into two groups: the *analytics,* who were reflective, studious, industrious, content to follow guidance, tending to group life; and the *creatives,* who were active, independent, aggressive, and "rejoiced in the conflict of ideas." "Dangerous women," he called the latter, and Washburn was the only woman he identified by name as belonging to that group: "Miss Washburn had been intrepid enough to invade the sacred precinct of the men's smoker at psychological meetings. Marching uninvited into its midst, she had sat down and lighted a cigar. None questioned her privilege to enjoy the smoker thereafter" (MacCracken 1950:70). The "creatives" on MacCracken's faculty were mostly women because, as he explained, "in a college for women, the men who accepted posts were likely to leave soon for other fields if creatively disposed" (1950:70). For Washburn, however, there was little choice but to remain at Vassar. Others with her reputation, ability, and preferences gravitated to graduate programs at preeminent research institutions. But they were men and, as a woman, she could not join them because of the stigma of her gender.

Washburn was not unaware of her particular professional status as a woman. She experienced the marginality imposed on women in science and would have understood the statement that "the cultural values bearing on women's place in the labor force generally and in the academic community particularly . . . represented both psychological and social barriers to women who desired careers" (Cole 1979:187).[13] On one occasion Washburn explicitly acknowledged her marginal status by aligning herself with a member of another disadvantaged group. Displaying the sharp wit for which she was well known, she commented on the irresponsible behavior of a prominent psychologist who had bungled his task of preparing a literature review for a special issue of the *Journal of Animal Behavior* :

Mr. Watson has given me much trouble, although you needn't tell him I said so; I have already dealt with him more in sorrow than in anger. . . . Mr. W. now tells me he simply neglected to answer my cards. . . . Inferior people, like Turner, who is a negro, and me, who am a woman, are willing to do this hack work as well as we can. Really superior people, like Wheeler, if they consent to do it at all, do it beautifully as they do everything else. Of the people in between, the less said the better. (to R. M. Yerkes, August 24, 1911, RMYP)

Washburn clearly did not believe that Turner was inferior; otherwise she would not have called on him to prepare reviews for the journal. Nor did she believe that she herself was inferior. Rather she was acknowledging that both she and Turner were likely to be considered professionally inferior because of her gender and his race.[14] Certainly they were being kept in their places. Though each was a recognized scholar in the field of comparative psychology, C. H. Turner was employed as a teacher at a black high school and she was limited to a women's college, whereas the offending reviewer, John B. Watson, held a professorship at Johns Hopkins and William Morton Wheeler was at Harvard. In the same line of correspondence, Washburn revealed her characteristic way of dealing with her situation:

Although [Watson's] reviews are full and valuable, he has given me more trouble by carelessness than all the others put together. . . . I smile to reflect what comments upon the feminine mind I should have made if I had been a man and my contributors women. However, even I am fallible on rare occasions. (October 14, 1911)

Because of her personal and intellectual strengths, Washburn was uniquely suited to contend with and persevere against what has been called "the triple penalty" imposed on women: the cultural perception that science is an inappropriate career for women, the belief that women are less competent scientists than men, and the actual discrimination against women in the scientific community.[15] Yet she did not address these issues directly. She proceeded as an autonomous individual, with a single-minded dedication to her own career. She refused to join organizations championing women's causes and never actively supported even the suffrage movement (Boring 1971:548).

In the 1920s Washburn vigorously opposed the introduction of special courses at Vassar designed to teach the "womanly arts" of family life, maternity, housewifery, nutrition, child study, and the like. She was not indifferent to the plight of women, but believed that women's education should be the same as that for men, rather than consisting of special efforts to train them for "women's work." Therefore, when President MacCracken proposed curricular reform, she accused him of "driving women back into the home, from the slavery of which education has helped us to escape" (MacCracken 1950:59). Washburn had fought for her freedom from domesticity and for professional recognition based on performance. MacCracken believed that "the battle was won" for women's equality of opportunity by then and that "only a cleaning up campaign was needed." Many well-informed people agreed with him.

Margaret Washburn, however, knew better—because of her own experience. In the first place, gender had restricted her opportunity for employment to a women's college. Furthermore, in a particularly galling example described in the next chapter, it had disbarred her from membership in a prominent group of experimental psychologists organized by her former adviser E. B. Titchener. Washburn's situation provided her with incontrovertible evidence that the notion of meritocracy in science—the belief that recognition, honor, and acceptance come to those who earn it—was for women little more than a myth.

CHAPTER 5

"A Little Hard on Ladies": Christine Ladd-Franklin's Challenge to Collegial Exclusion

A letter appearing in the *New York Times* in December 1921 assailed the American Academy of Arts and Letters for excluding women from its ranks. "Isn't it rather absurd," Christine Ladd-Franklin wrote, "that Edith Wharton, for instance, who is without question the most distinguished American in the realm of letters, should not have been invited to join a self-constituted body of 'immortals'? " (December 13, 1921). She went on to entertain the idea that there was perhaps more justification for a male authors "club" if that was what the members preferred but that the members of a group who "arrogate to themselves a name of such special connotation as 'Academy' . . . show themselves very lacking in good taste at least, if they exclude women."

Ladd-Franklin drew an unfavorable comparison between the men of letters and men in the sciences by claiming that it was

a long time since other organizations have found any reason for not admitting women. The scientific societies for instance, have not only admitted them but have treated them with all deserved honor: Professor Calkins of Wellesley has been President of both the Psychological Association and the Philosophical Association, and this very month the Psychological Association meeting at Princeton will be presided over by President Washburn of Vassar. Does not the Academy of Arts and Letters (which ought if anything to be further advanced in the humanities than the plain scientists) feel that it is rather old fashioned? (*New York Times*, December 13, 1921)

For Ladd-Franklin, who was by then in her seventies, the public expression of feminist sentiments was an ingrained habit. Thirty years earlier, for example, she had reviewed a new edition of *A Vindication of the Rights of Women* in which she heartily endorsed Mary Wollstonecraft's admonition to women that "their first duty is to themselves as rational creatures" (Ladd-Franklin 1891a:164). This stance characterized Ladd-Franklin's views on women as she aired them repeatedly in the pages of the weekly magazine *The Nation* during the late 1880s and the 1890s in book reviews, brief topical articles, and letters to the editor.[1] She belonged to the pioneering generation of women collegians and scientists and spoke movingly in one of her articles of the plight of these intellectually aspiring women: "No man can ever fully realize the feeling of isolation and repression which was the lot, up to thirty years ago of those few active minded women who were afflicted with an unnatural desire to aid in the accumulation of the world's store of exact knowledge" (Ladd-Franklin 1896b:236).

In an article written to commemorate the twenty-fifth anniversary of her alma mater, Vassar College, she reflected with a touch of sarcasm on how recently the intellectual inferiority of women had been the generally accepted view: "Twenty five years ago it was honestly supposed, no doubt, by most people that the feminine cortex was of so soft and flabby a texture as to be quite incapable of following solid trains of thought" (Ladd-Franklin 1890:483). For Ladd-Franklin, now that women's capability at the college level was a matter of record, it was time to remove the barriers to their pursuit of advanced work: "What remains is to make the post collegiate education equally easy of access to women. . . . What possible reason can Columbia College, or Clark University, or the Johns Hopkins urge for not throwing open their post-graduate courses to women?" (484).

There were two other issues that Ladd-Franklin addressed as vitally important to women's well-being: economic independence and self-sacrifice. She was as strongly opposed to the latter as she as in favor of the former. To Ladd-Franklin, "it

Christine Ladd-Franklin (1847–1930). (Courtesy of the Rare Book and Manuscript Library, Columbia University.)

was perfectly plain that nothing is more hazardous to the happiness and to the permanence of marriage, or more destructive to the feeling of equality that ought to pervade the married state, than for young girls to feel, in even a slight degree, that they are expected to marry as the only natural mode of providing for themselves" (Ladd-Franklin 1891b:53). In order to remove this possibility, Ladd-Franklin exhorted "the friends of women . . . to concern themselves with opening the more lucrative professions to them, and to seeing to it that they obtain equal wages with men for equal work." She also counseled women against turning their property over to their husbands when they married, observing that "it is only to the extent to which women have been able to keep the control of their property in their own hands that they have been able to preserve their independence" (Ladd-Franklin 1896a:91).

Ladd-Franklin flatly rejected the widely held opinion that self-sacrifice was a virtue toward which women should strive. On the contrary, she expressed the view that "the principal causes why women often carry on their lives on a lower plane than they might attain to are the trivialness and the inordinate self-sacrifice to which they fall victim" (Ladd-Franklin 1889:327). "No nice young girl," she ruefully observed, "is capable of resisting the claims of other members of the family upon her sympathy and her actual practical aid in the thousand and one events of the day." And, in her opinion, it was not only girls whose lives were adversely affected: "Many women are . . . of so self-sacrificing a temperament that they need to be artificially guarded against themselves."

Over the years, Christine Ladd-Franklin zealously continued to champion the cause of women in matters such as equal access to education and the professions and their right to the vote. It is not surprising then that in 1921 she took up her cudgel against the American Academy of Arts and Letters for excluding women. However, her letter to the editor contains a curious oversight. In fact, knowing the circumstances, one might even charge Ladd-Franklin with being less than candid in her account.

It was true that the APA had moved to admit women to membership almost from its beginning and had even elected two women presidents. However, another group of psychologists, well known to Ladd-Franklin, who called themselves "the Experimentalists" had by that time been in existence for over fifteen years and had always maintained a ban on women members. Ladd-Franklin strenuously protested this policy but had been rebuffed in her attempts to change it. Perhaps this explains why she conveniently chose to ignore the group in her letter to the editor in her assertion that it had been a long time since scientific societies had found any reason for not admitting women.

The story of the uncollegial attitude of the experimental psychologists who were men toward the women in their field does bear telling. Among other things, it throws into sharp relief the very different experience of men and women in that area of the discipline. The tale begins in 1904. In February of that year, Cornell psychologist E. B. Titchener wrote to his Harvard colleague Hugo Münsterberg, voicing a widely acknowledged need of scientists engaged in research—to be able to talk shop with peers informally and on a regular basis:

For many years I wanted an experimental club—no officers, the men moving about and handling [apparatus], the visited lab to do the work, no women, smoking allowed, plenty of frank criticism and discussions, the whole atmosphere experimental, the youngsters taken in on an equality with the men who have arrived. (February 1, 1904, HMP)

Titchener envisioned bringing together a group of colleagues who would participate in an informal communication system—from which women would be excluded.

Why exclude women? Presumably because in that era men could not feel at ease and fully free to enjoy each other's company in the presence of women. Further, Titchener, like most men of his generation, found it difficult if not impossible to see women as genuine colleagues. This is understandable given that the accepted gender roles assigned women a status both

Edward Bradford Titchener (1867–1927). (Courtesy of the Cornell University Archives.)

separate and distinctly subordinate to that of men. The collegial role, in contrast, is one of exchange among equals (Reskin 1978). Titchener, a transplanted Englishman and a traditionalist, not surprisingly was incapable of setting aside the prescribed *gender* role in which men were dominant over women for the *collegial* role, which required an egalitarian relationship among women and men. Whatever his reasons, the effect on women experimental psychologists was clear; his proposal cut them off from an immensely important resource for advancing their careers as scientists.

Why Titchener wanted another professional organization for psychologists when the American Psychological Association had already been in existence for twelve years also requires some explanation. Titchener had had his quarrels with the APA, resigning in protest in the 1890s when the organization failed to expel one of its members whom he believed guilty of plagiarism. But it has been suggested that there were two more fundamental reasons why he found the APA uncongenial for his purposes, reasons relating to the content as well as the format of the yearly meetings.[2]

For Titchener "truly scientific psychology was pure introspection. The psychologist established the conditions of consciousness—no more or less" (Bjork 1983:80). This straight and narrow approach to psychology limited the acceptable subject matter for a professional meeting, as Titchener saw it, to "generalized, human, adult, normal, experimental psychology" (Boring 1938:410). However, interests other than those Titchener considered to be experimental psychology were beginning to dominate the APA. Much to Titchener's consternation, philosophy and other topics—mental testing, child study, abnormal psychology, and animal psychology—were attracting the attention of American psychologists and occupying an ever more prominent place in the program of APA's annual meeting (Goodwin 1985).

In addition to the content of the APA meetings being not sufficiently experimental, the time allotted to presentations was too short, the apparatus used in the investigations absent, and the results obscured by the lack of charts and diagrams. As Titchener saw it, if such conditions persisted "it would seem that the drift of the Association must continue in the non-experimental direction" (cited in Goodwin 1985:385).

These objections prompted Titchener to carry out his plan for an experimental club and for more than twenty years, until his death in 1927, he directed and dominated the group, which included the heads of the most prestigious psychological laboratories in North America. Each spring Titchener's society would meet at an Eastern university—Cornell, Clark, Yale, Harvard, Pennsylvania, Princeton, Johns Hopkins, Wesleyan, and Columbia all served as sites for one or more meetings. The director of the psychological laboratory at the institution where the meeting was held served as host to the invited heads of other laboratories and to some of their junior colleagues and advanced graduate students. During the meetings "the youngsters" made important contacts with "the men who [had] arrived" and current research was discussed as well as issues of general interest and significance to the psychological profession.

At a memorable meeting in 1917, the final session took place on the day that the United States declared war on Germany. The Experimentalists turned the session over to a discussion of "the relations of psychology to national defense" and at the end appointed a committee to explore the topic further (Yerkes 1921:7). In effect, Titchener's elite club assumed the responsibility for planning how American psychologists would become involved in the war effort.

Titchener's ban on women was rigorously maintained from the beginning of the group in 1904 until its reorganization in 1929. Although Titchener was without question an imposing, formidable figure, there is good reason to believe that he was not single-handedly fighting to keep women out of the group. There was no particular outcry from the men when his policy toward women was first announced. In fact, the correspondence Titchener received early in 1904 as he consulted with colleagues about the proposed society was largely silent on the issue. It reveals more concern over whether the country contained enough psychologists to support another organization and the possible negative consequences for the APA of a rival group. Münsterberg, for example, sent a two-page typewritten letter to Titchener in which there is no mention of the women issue whereas he discussed the competition with APA at length (January 30, 1904, EBTP).

References to the exclusion of women appear in only three letters to Titchener during that period: two raised questions about the policy and one wholeheartedly endorsed it. E. C. Sanford, Milicent Shinn's favorite cousin and Mary Calkins' friend and mentor, voiced concern:

The question with regard to women in the association is a poser. Several of them on scientific grounds have full right to be there and might feel hurt (in a general impersonal way) if women are not asked. On the other hand they would undoubtedly interfere with the smoking and to a certain extent with the general freedom of a purely masculine assembly. Would it be possible to give them also the chance to say whether they would like to come—assuring them by a personal note that transactions would not come off except in a partially smoke-charged atmosphere? (January 19, 1904, EBTP)

August Kirschmann, a psychologist at the University of Toronto, while basically agreeing with Titchener's proposal for a group, also questioned the policy on women: "I find it a little hard on ladies, who take an interest in Experimental Psychology if we exclude them altogether" (March 5, 1904, EBTP).

On the other hand, although he expressed regret over the exclusion of "a number of very capable experimentalists," Lightner Witmer, at the University of Pennsylvania, wrote in support of banning women from the proposed society:

I am quite positive in my objection to inviting women. . . . I am sure from my experience, that you cannot run an informal meeting of men and women. . . . We want a small vigorous association where we can speak our minds with perfect freedom. . . . The larger and more heterogeneous the organization the more likely is vigorous discussion to be misinterpreted and to be taken as an offence [sic] by individuals who may happen to be attacked. I think that the presence of women in the organization adds greatly to this danger, owing to the personal attitude which they usually take even in scientific discussions. I favor a small association, no invited guests, and no women members. (January 25, 1904, EBTP)

These very few references to "the woman question" Titchener raised could be interpreted as tacit approval of his policy of exclusion. And after its formation, there are only two recorded occurrences both quite early, that might signify resistance to the policy from within the group.

The first incident—essentially a mere gesture—involved James Rowland Angell of the University of Chicago, who had a reputation for being outspoken in his insistence on equality of opportunity for women (Rosenberg 1982:62–68). Although Angell was invited to the first meeting of the Experimentalists at Cornell, he did not attend. He did, however, submit a paper and perhaps not coincidentally, it was written by a woman, his graduate student Matilde Castro. The other incident occurred in 1907 at the University of Pennsylvania meeting. Titchener, later writing to Münsterberg about the event, described how James Leuba, a professor at Bryn Mawr (a nearby women's college), had sent some of his students to attend the meeting. Titchener remarked that the "girls" were "promptly turned out" and dismissed the incident as "sheer misunderstanding" (February 29, 1908, HMP).

While men psychologists expressed few objections and offered little or no resistance to Titchener's policy on women, what of women experimental psychologists? How did they react to being excluded from Titchener's club? At least some of Titchener's women graduate students adjusted to it by eavesdropping on the proceedings. E. G. Boring described one such episode which occurred at his first meeting in 1911 when he was a graduate student at Cornell. Two of Titchener's graduate students, Boring's future wife Lucy Day and another woman, "secreted themselves in a next room with the door just ajar to hear what unexpurgated male psychology was like." Reportedly "they came through unscathed" (Boring

1967:322). Boring also recounted another story, confessing it had never been verified "that two women graduate students once hid under a table, covered with a green baize cloth . . . while the Experimentalists went on" (Boring 1967:322).

Some of Titchener's many women graduate students may have resorted to hiding under tables or behind doors to get a sense of what transpired at the meetings. What about the women who were already established in the discipline? The most prominent women were the three who were among a group of fifty psychologists ranked as the most eminent in the field in 1903: Mary Whiton Calkins, Margaret Floy Washburn, and Christine Ladd-Franklin (Cattell and Cattell 1933).

Ladd-Franklin, widely known for her theory of color vision and an internationally recognized authority on the topic of vision, was appreciably older than both Calkins and Washburn and was twenty years Titchener's senior. She was by far the most outspoken of the three women on the issue of women's rights, and she alone among them directly and repeatedly challenged Titchener for his discriminatory practices.

Their different childhood experiences and temperaments may account for the different responses these women made to a common problem. Ladd-Franklin, unlike Calkins and Washburn, had a mother who embraced feminist ideas and impressed them on her daughter from an early age. When Christine was not quite five years old, for example, her mother Augusta took her to hear a popular lecturer, reformer, and women's rights advocate. Augusta later enthusiastically described the event and its impact on her young daughter in a letter to her sister Riar: "I went last evening to Mrs. Oakes-Smith's lecture with Kitty for company . . . and had a fine time. . . . Kitty expects to be a lecturer as she was so pleased, with what she heard, when not sleeping" (November 16, n.y., CLF&FFP). Also, apparently less bound by the late Victorian code of ladylike behavior than Calkins and Washburn, Ladd-Franklin became legendary for her assertiveness in interactions with colleagues, men and women alike. To at least one psychologist, a younger man, she "appeared a remarkable woman" when seen "at close range" because of "her keen logical mind and her cheerful aggressiveness" (Woodworth 1930:307).

Christine Ladd-Franklin's parents were both descendants of established New England families. During her early childhood, she lived with her parents and younger brother in New York City where her father was a merchant. In 1853 they moved to Windsor, Connecticut, where her mother's relatives lived and her sister was born the following year. When her mother died of pneumonia in spring 1860, the grief-stricken twelve-year-old was separated from her father and siblings, spent time with various relatives, and for a while attended school in Portsmouth, New Hampshire, where her paternal grandmother lived.

A precocious and avid student, Ladd-Franklin began very early to nurture a hope that, although a girl, she might find a means to continue her education beyond secondary school. When she was sixteen, she recorded in her diary with great excitement the news of a proposed college for women in New York state, the first to offer a course of study comparable to the men's colleges: "I am crying for very joy. I have been reading an account of the Vassar female college that is to be. The glorious emancipation proclamation for woman has gone forth and now no power can put her back in her former state. . . . Oh! I must go. I must prevail upon my father to send me. . . . Let me study diligently now as preparation" (Pre-Vassar Diary, March 27, 1863, CLFP).[3]

Ladd-Franklin's father gave her the opportunity to spend the next two years studying at a coeducational academy in Wilbraham, Massachusetts, taking the same courses that were preparing the boys there to enter colleges such as Harvard. During these two intellectually stimulating years and the next discouraging one (when she was back home in Connecticut looking for a teaching job), she filled the pages of her diary with her hopes and fears about her chances of going to Vassar some day.

In summer 1866 a diary entry describes how she had won her grandmother over to her side on the college issue:

I have gained an important point with my grandma. She says she thinks Auntie ought to send me to Vassar. She objected that at the end of four years I should be too old to get married. I assured her that it would afford me great pleasure to entangle a husband but there was no one [in] the place who would have me or whom I would have and out of this place I was destined never to go, gave her statistics of the great excess of females in New England and proved that as I was decidedly *not* handsome my chances were very small. Therefore since I could not find a husband to support me I must support myself and to do so I needed an education. Grandma succumbed. (July 23, 1866)

Her father was apparently not so easily swayed by her arguments, as she confided to her diary a few days later. In her desperation, she considered challenging his authority: "Wonder what would be the consequences of rebellion? Auntie consents to send me to Vassar and father does not allow me to go" (July 28, 1866). The diary gives no hint of how the father was eventually converted on the Vassar matter, agreeing to accept a loan from his deceased wife's sister, but in August this gleeful entry appears: "Vassar! Land of my longing! Mine at last. In a month I shall pace the spacious corridors and busy myself in the volumes of forgotten lore at Vassar!" (August 10, 1866). And then even she was forced to admit some uneasiness about the wisdom of the radical experiment she was to undertake: "Does it really seem so beautiful as I thought it would? Is it really for the best? I confess I have misgivings—everyone is so opposed to it."

In fall 1866 Christine Ladd became a member of the second entering class of Vassar College. She was prevented from returning to Vassar the next academic year presumably because her father was in financial difficulty. However, additional funds provided by her aunt enabled her to reenter Vassar and to complete her degree in 1868–69. At Vassar her primary academic interests were in science and mathematics, and for almost a decade following her graduation she earned a living by teaching these subjects in secondary schools in Pennsylvania, Massachusetts, and New York. Teaching was a vocation she soon grew to loathe, as she noted in her diary in January

Christine Ladd as a student at Vassar, 1860s. (Courtesy of the Rare Book and Manuscript Library, Columbia University.)

1872: "Sunday evening is the most miserable time of all the week. The burdens of the morrow look impossible to be born. Teaching I hate with a perfect hatred. . . . I shall not be able to endure it another year" (Vassar Diary, January 28, 1872, CLFP). Yet she continued to teach for several more years, while also studying and publishing papers in mathematics.

Soon after Johns Hopkins University opened, she applied for admission there to take up advanced work in mathematics. This new institution was to be dedicated to research work and graduate study, the first of its kind in the United States modeled after the German university. The authorities there were reluctant, however, to offer the school's unique opportunities to women. Only at the bidding of a professor of mathematics at Johns Hopkins, who was familiar with her mathematical papers, was she permitted to attend his lectures—but no others—in the 1878–79 academic year (see Hawkins 1960:263–65).

As time passed the recognition of her extraordinary intellectual ability made it possible for her to attend other courses at the university, and she was even awarded the stipend of a fellow, although because of her gender she was not given the title. For the same reason, she was not awarded a Ph.D. in mathematics and logic even though by 1882 she had fulfilled all of the requirements. Johns Hopkins did grant her the doctorate belatedly in 1926 on the occasion of its fiftieth anniversary. Ladd-Franklin, then nearly eighty years old, was there in person to accept the degree she had earned forty-four years earlier.

Soon after completing her work at Johns Hopkins, she married Fabian Franklin, a young member of the mathematics faculty there. In the next two years, when she was in her midthirties, she bore two children—a son, who lived only a few days, and a daughter Margaret, born in August 1884.

The topic of vision had captured Ladd-Franklin's interest by 1887. In that year, she made her entry into psychology with the publication of a paper on binocular vision (Ladd-Franklin 1887). Her husband's sabbatical leave from Johns Hopkins in 1891–92 gave the couple an opportunity to spend a year in Europe, where Ladd-Franklin pursued her new interest. In Germany she managed to circumvent the official policy that excluded women from enrolling in the universities. Winning the support of one of the foremost German psychologists, G. E. Müller, she carried out experimental work in vision in his laboratory at Göttingen. In addition, Ladd-Franklin traveled to Berlin where she worked in the laboratory of the renowned scientist Hermann von Helmholtz and attended the lectures of an adherent of Helmholtz's theory of color vision, Arthur König. By the end of her year abroad, she had developed her own theory of color vision, an evolutionarily based model that she presented to the International Congress of Psychology in London. It was a theory that she was to defend and promote tirelessly for the rest of her life—a span of almost forty years.

Christine Ladd-Franklin's employment after her marriage was limited to a part-time lectureship in logic and psychology from 1904 to 1909 at Johns Hopkins and, after the Franklins moved to New York City in 1910, a similar appointment at Columbia University. The evidence suggests that she had to wage a strenuous campaign to obtain even these marginal appointments which amounted to teaching one or two courses per year, in some instances without pay. In marked contrast with many other women psychologists who married, for example Ethel Puffer, Ladd-Franklin remained scientifically active over the years, developing her theory of color vision and conducting research on the topic. She attended and gave papers at American psychological meetings as well as at several international congresses. Her work was published in numerous journals, and her book, which was a collection of her papers on vision spanning more than three decades (Ladd-Franklin 1929), appeared shortly before her death in 1930. Through the years she carried on a brisk correspondence with many scholars in the fields of logic and psychology including E. B. Titchener.

Ladd-Franklin began corresponding with Titchener as soon as the young Englishman, who taken his Ph.D. with Wundt in Leipzig, arrived in the United States. In 1892 he began as assistant professor of psychology at Cornell where he set up his own laboratory, hiding "his mere twenty-five years behind a bushy beard and a formidable manner. During the thirty-five years that he taught at Ithaca that beard grew no scantier, and the manner changed only to become more formalized" (Adams

1931:441). Both Titchener and Ladd-Franklin became legendary for their dominating personalities, and while Titchener was a stickler in matters of decorum, neither he nor Ladd-Franklin was apt to mince words.

When Titchener was in his midforties and Ladd-Franklin in her midsixties, an exchange of letters on Titchener's policy of excluding women from the meetings of the Experimentalists began. Her reaction was initially one of incredulity. This soon gave way to indignation, and by 1914 her response could fairly be described as one of outrage. In 1912 she wrote ingenuously to Titchener: "I am particularly anxious to bring my views up, once in a while, for hand-to-hand discussion before experts, and just now I have especially a paper which I should like very much to read before your meeting of experimental psychologists. I hope you will not say nay!" (undated, CLF&FFP). Titchener's reply has been lost, but it appears he did reply with a "nay" because Ladd-Franklin's next letter to him begins: "I am shocked to know that you are still—at this year—excluding women from your meeting of experimental psychologists. It is such a very old-fashioned standpoint!" (undated, CLF&FFP).

She told him how irrational he was, in that year's meeting which would be held at Clark University, to "include in your invitation . . . the students of G. Stanley Hall, who are not in the least experimentalists and exclude the women who are doing particularly good work in the experimental laboratory of Prof. Baird." And she assailed him for his tactic of excluding women from a scientific meeting on social grounds: "Have your smokers separated if you like (tho I for one always smoke when I am in fashionable society), but a scientific meeting (however personal) is a public affair, and it is not open to you to leave out a class of fellow workers without extreme discourtesy" (undated, CLF&FFP).

Although Titchener refused to budge before Ladd-Franklin's arguments on the issue of women at the Clark meeting in 1912, she achieved token success two years later when the meetings were held at Columbia. By that time she was living in New York City and teaching occasional courses in logic and color vision at Columbia. In her letter to Titchener shortly before the April meeting, she referred to a compliment he had paid her by including her in the group of psychologists that had "some logic in them." She then rebuked him for continuing to exclude her from his club: "Is this then a good time, my dear Professor Titchener, for you to hold to the mediaeval attitude of not admitting me to your coming psychological conference in New York—at my very door? So unconscientious, so immoral,—worse than that—so unscientific!" (March 21, 1914, CLF&FFP).

Despite his obstinacy, Titchener was affected by her verbal assaults. He wrote to Harvard psychologist Robert M. Yerkes shortly before the Columbia meeting:

I am not sure that we had better not disintegrate! I have been pestered by abuse by Mrs. Ladd-Franklin for not having women at the meetings, and she threatens to make various scenes in person and in print. Possibly she will succeed in breaking us up, and forcing us to meet—like rabbits—in some dark place underground. (April 2, 1914, RMYP)

Boring reported that Christine Ladd-Franklin did come to one session at the Columbia meeting but he added "tradition was kept supreme at the others" (1938:414). And for another fifteen years, to all accounts, tradition would be kept supreme until, after Titchener's death, the group reorganized and elected in 1929 its first women members: June Etta Downey[4] and Margaret Floy Washburn.

Why were the remaining two eminent women psychologists—Calkins and Ladd-Franklin—not made members at that time? Calkins was not included presumably because her interests had turned from psychology to philosophy by then. Although Ladd-Franklin was still keenly interested in psychology, she frankly overawed the male psychologists of her day and it seems likely that her personality was the stumbling block that kept her from being invited into the group.

Of the three most outstanding women psychologists, Wash-

Psychology Dinner In Honor Of President James R. Angell
On The Thirtieth Anniversary of His Appointment As Professor of Psychology
Members of the Society of Experimental Psychologists and Guests
Faculty Club, Yale University, April 4, 1935

Top row: (Left to right): J. A. McGeoch, Missouri; H. W. Nissen, Yale; L. P. Herrington, Yale; C. F. Jacobsen, Yale; C. Landis, New York Psychiatric Institute; L. Carmichael, Brown; A. B. Crawford, Yale; M. Bentley, Cornell; W. S. Hunter, Clark, Chairman-Elect S. E. P.

Third row: E. S. Robinson, Yale; H. M. Halverson, Yale; J. Peterson, George Peabody College; A. T. Poffenberger, Jr., Columbia; K. Koffka, Smith; C. L. Hull, Yale; K. M. Dallenbach, Cornell; H. S. Langfeld, Princeton; H. M. Johnson, American University; H. L. Hollingworth, Barnard College; C. C. Pratt, Harvard; S. W. Fernberger, University of Pennsylvania, — Secretary S. E. P.

Second row: A. Gesell, Yale; K. Lewin, Cornell; M. Wertheimer, New School, New York; M. F. Washburn, Vassar; President Angell; W. R. Miles, Yale, Chairman S. E. P.; R. Dodge, Yale; R. S. Woodworth, Columbia; E. G. Boring, Harvard.

Bottom row: B. M. Castner, Yale; J. W. Tilton, Yale; L. W. Doob, Yale; E. G. Wever, Princeton; G. R. Wendt, Yale; R. T. Ross, Yale; A. W. Melton, Yale; D. G. Marquis, Yale.

Margaret Floy Washburn and the Society of Experimental Psychologists at Yale University, 1935. (Courtesy of Yale University Library.)

burn had perhaps the most grounds to be offended by Titchener's exclusionary policy. Not only was she his first graduate student; she also went on to become an outstanding scientist in the field of experimental psychology and was the second woman elected to the prestigious National Academy of Sciences (see chapter 4). How she felt about Titchener's exclusion of women from the Experimentalists cannot be determined from her correspondence, but she was clearly alienated from the man. When Ladd-Franklin wrote to her shortly after Titchener's death asking her as his closest representative to write an obituary, Washburn replied:

I never had any quarrel with him or personal grievance against him, but I never either liked or admired him, and have had for years little agreement with his views. I have not seen him, I suppose, for twenty years, nor corresponded with him. I can think of few persons to whom I have felt less near than I have always felt to him. (August 16, 1927, CLF&FFP)

In the same vein, Washburn wrote a few months later to a colleague whom she had known since their graduate school days at Cornell: "Do you know that next to Dr. Cattell you are now my oldest surviving psychological friend?" Squeezed into the space above that line was added the afterthought: "(The 'now' is superfluous: E. B. T. wasn't a friend)" (to Walter Pillsbury, March 28, 1928, WBPP).

Mary Whiton Calkins, who started out as an experimental psychologist, in later years shifted her interest to philosophical work on the self (see chapter 1). Concerned over discrimination against women, yet unwilling to join a public crusade against Titchener, she expressed her view to Ladd-Franklin in summer 1912 after the Clark meeting:

As to the experimental psychologists: I of course share your regret at their attitude toward women. In fact, I have . . . spoken of the matter in years past to Dr. Titchener and to Dr. Münsterberg (the latter, I think favors their entrance). I feel the freer to speak because I no longer count myself an experimenter: but you, Miss Gamble, Miss Washburn, Miss Cook, and several others should of course be invited. At the same time I doubt the wisdom of a public protest on the part of those who are shut out. It seems to be sufficiently a side-issue to be left to time or to protestants from within. (August 14, n.y., CLF&FFP)

Christine Ladd-Franklin however was not content to let the matter be resolved by the passage of time or by advocates of women within the Experimentalists. She sensed, as perhaps Calkins did not, how durable the policy on women would prove to be and how few friends of women could be counted within the ranks of Titchener's group. Even though Ladd-Franklin would persist at least until 1916 in her protests to Titchener and others, her efforts to open the doors to women did not succeed.

What were the consequences of the systematic exclusion of women experimentalists from Titchener's group? Women who were already established psychologists when the society was founded, such as Calkins, Ladd-Franklin, and Washburn, were perhaps less adversely affected than the next generation of women who aspired to enter the field and were denied the informal contacts with prominent men that Titchener's club provided. Such contacts proved invaluable to young men launching careers in the field. For example, it was through meetings with the Experimentalists that the young John B. Watson, who later gained fame for his behaviorist interpretation of psychology, came to the attention of Titchener and other established psychologists (see Larson and Sullivan 1965).[5]

Although officially permitted membership in the reorganized Society of Experimental Psychologists, as it was renamed two years after Titchener's death, women—already numerous in psychology—were never well represented in the society's ranks.[6] The reasons for their continued absence remain a matter of conjecture. It is possible that a bias against women may have been operating in the election procedure. Or, women may have chosen not to enter experimental psychology, perceiving it as inhospitable to women because Titchener's group had for so long remained an all-male club. Still another plausible explanation is that the prolonged exclusion had thwarted women's achievement in experimental psychology to such a degree that they were not considered qualified for membership.

Whatever the reasons, their absence from the society is a matter of fact. This is strikingly documented in a photo of the Society of Experimental Psychologists taken as they assembled for their meeting at Princeton University in 1947, twenty years after Titchener's death. The photo shows a group of thirty-nine psychologists, all of them men, embodying perfectly Titchener's original idea of "an experimental club [with] no women."

PART TWO

COLLECTIVE PORTRAIT OF
THE FIRST GENERATION

CHAPTER 6

Origins, Education, and Life-Styles

In the preceding chapters we have considered several pervasive themes in the lives of early women psychologists. We elaborated the experiences of a few individuals in relation to these themes to show how women's experience was different from that of men in the discipline. In this chapter and the next, we consider the first generation of American women psychologists as a group. Who were the women choosing to place themselves in a situation so problematical for their identity? Where did they come from? How did they proceed? And with what outcomes for their lives? In this collective portrait, we describe the group, examining their origins, education, and lifestyles in this chapter and their careers and contributions in the next. Several women whose lives illustrate particular aspects of the discussion are featured in individual cameo portraits, presented in appendix A.

As stated in the introduction, we are calling the "first generation" those women who entered the field by 1906. This includes women who had joined the American Psychological Association by that date or listed psychology as their subject field in the 1906 edition of *American Men of Science*. Using these criteria, we found twenty-five women who comprise the first generation of women psychologists. Their names and dates of entry are given in table 6.1. Biographical details for many of them may be found in standard sources, as listed in appendix B, and in Furumoto and Scarborough (1986).

Table 6.1. Women Who Were Members of American Psychological Association or Who Listed Their Field as Psychology in *American Men of Science* by 1906

			Date Joined APA
Adams, Elizabeth Kemper	—	APA	1905
Allen, Jessie Blount (Mrs. Werrett W. Charters)	AMS[a]	APA	1906
Bagley (Mrs. William C.), Florence MacLean Winger	AMS	—	
Calkins, Mary Whiton	AMS	APA	1893
Case, Mary Sophia	AMS	—	
Franklin (Mrs. Fabian), Christine Ladd	AMS	APA	1893
Gamble, Eleanor Acheson McCulloch	AMS	APA	1898
Gordon, Kate (Mrs. Ernest Carroll Moore)	AMS	APA	1905
Hamlin, Alice Julia (Mrs. Edgar L. Hinman)	AMS	APA	1896
McKeag, Anna Jane	AMS	APA	1908[b]
Martin, Lillien Jane	AMS	APA	1899
Moore (Mrs. J. Percy), Kathleen Carter	AMS	APA	1904
Norsworthy, Naomi	AMS	APA	1905
Prichard, Margaret S.	—	APA	1905
Puffer, Ethel Dench (Mrs. Benjamin A. Howes)	AMS	APA	1898
Rousmaniere, Frances H. (Mrs. Arthur S. Dewing)	—	APA	1906
Rowland, Eleanor Harris (Mrs. Harry Wembridge)	AMS[a]	APA	1905
Shinn, Milicent Washburn	AMS	—	
Smith, Margaret Kiever	AMS	APA	1902
Smith, Theodate Louise	AMS	APA	1905
Squire (Mrs. William N.), Carrie Ranson	AMS	—	
Talbot, Ellen Bliss	—	APA	1899
Thompson, Helen Bradford (Mrs. Paul Woolley)	AMS	APA	1902
Washburn, Margaret Floy	AMS	APA	1894
Williams, Mabel Clare (Mrs. T. W. Kemmerer)	AMS	APA	1907[b]

Note: Women listed alphabetically by name used when first listed in APA or *AMS*.

[a]First listed in second edition of *AMS* (1910).
[b]Elected to APA after listing in *AMS*.

This group cannot be called a birth cohort because the women differed greatly in age, ranging from twenty-three to fifty-nine years old in 1906.[1] Nevertheless they constitute a coherent *professional* cohort: each woman acquired her experience with scientific psychology in the preceding fifteen years. It is in this sense that we see them as a "generation." They entered psychology at a particular time and therefore shared a set of common experiences. The age range may be explained by the fact that it was only around 1890 that psychology became a distinct field of study in America. The older women in our group moved into the field in their middle years; the younger ones came to it earlier in their educational experience. Succeeding generations of women in psychology entered with several important differences. They were more likely to be introduced to psychology during their college years and found it possible to move directly into the graduate training programs that became more accessible to women by the turn of the century. Further, these later women encountered a somewhat different situation in psychology itself.

Once institutions offering graduate study in psychology opened to women, they seized the opportunity. This sudden influx of women into a new science we attribute to the convergence of two important developments occurring about the same time—the opening of graduate schools to women and the introduction of psychology as a distinct academic discipline. New graduate departments were "anxious to build themselves up" (Woody 1929, 2:334), and psychology was anxious to build itself up. Both graduate programs and psychology needed new recruits. This situation allowed women to consider psychology as an option and to enjoy a certain degree of acceptance in the field. It may explain why women were more strongly represented in psychology than in the other sciences of that period.[2]

Psychology began to stabilize as a discipline in the years following 1900. Growing recognition of the field as a science and as an academic discipline led to a shift away from concerns over its establishment to a new set of concerns focusing on its prestige. As one historian writes: "Relentless concern for full-scale development, and for stature . . . emerged as the prevalent characteristic of the psychologists' movement toward professionalization in the years between 1904 and 1917" (Camfield 1973:70-71). The first generation of women, then, entered psychology during its formative years, when the focus of its leaders was on expansion. They were admitted to graduate programs, which served as the entry vehicle, because they could swell the numbers and generate studies that would establish the legitimacy of the new science. The power structure of the professional group was still in flux, but there were some sympathetic men in leadership positions who acknowledged women's potential and were willing to sponsor them. Later women encountered a somewhat different situation, one more similar to that faced by women attempting to enter the better-established sciences in the late nineteenth century.[3]

Another difference setting first-generation women apart from their successors was employment opportunity. In the early years, academic institutions were the only place for a professional psychologist to earn a living. Early in the twentieth century, however, psychology began to expand, offering other types of employment. Though all of the first generation began with careers in academia, several of the women subsequently moved into applied work settings, both by choice and of necessity when they found academic opportunities scarce. Later women, however, were likely to undertake *initial* employment in a wide range of settings: schools, clinics and hospitals, businesses, governmental and public service agencies.

ORIGINS

Psychology's first women were ethnically and socially homogeneous. They came from the fortunate middle class that became a dominant feature of American life in the nineteenth century. Colorfully described by Burton Bledstein (1976), this social group was a broad class, delimited by neither income nor occupation, but standing between a small aristocracy and the laboring class. The middle class was characterized by a zeal for self-improvement through education and vocation. Its members combined high ambition with great energy and were "competitive, active, bold, brave, and even reckless. . . . [They] invented means . . . opened doors of opportunity" (27). They were also, however, concerned with establishing "universal standards for moral and civil behavior" so their adventuresomeness was linked with other somewhat contradictory traits. Further, they were organizers: "punctual, industrious, mathematical, and impersonal" (27). This state of mind, which represented a distinctive set of attitudes, emerged in the North and spread westward, directing much of nineteenth-century activity. It also describes rather nicely the personal characteristics of many of the women we are considering.

The first women psychologists were native white women descended from old colonial families with English roots. Nearly all came from small towns in the Northeast or Midwest.[4] Generally the families had strong Protestant affiliations and the daughters continued in the religious tradition of their ancestors.[5] The women were raised in stable families that often included considerable interaction with extended family networks. Most had several siblings, and many experienced the early death of one or more of these. The fathers were mainly professionals, including several clergymen and physicians; some were prosperous businessmen. The mothers followed the typical pattern for middle-class wives, being devoted to family and domestic activities, though many had had unusual educational opportunities for women of their time and several had been teachers before marriage.

These parents formed a particular subset of the emerging middle class. They were relatively well educated and had strong cultural interests. More important, they were among those who increasingly recognized that education for daughters represented both an economic and an intellectual advantage. Their daughters, who chose to seek advanced education and careers, were acting on values that reflected their parents' belief in personal advancement. However, they were operating also in a cultural milieu that attempted to confine women's activities to the domestic domain. Thus although they defied convention by challenging accepted roles, they could do so with great determination and confidence because of their supportive families.

While the families of origin were solidly middle class, most apparently did not provide the financial resources to support their daughter's collegiate study. Barbara Solomon has pointed out that paying for college expenses was likely to place a severe burden on families in the social class most inclined to encourage advanced education. Financing a college education was a major investment: in 1890 the average salary of a teacher was $250; of a minister, $900; and of a physician, $1200. In that same year, room, board, and tuition at Wellesley College was $350 (Solomon 1985:65).

However, adequate financial resources were not a problem for some of the women, whose families were comfortably secure, if not wealthy. Washburn, for example, spoke of her great-grandfather's success as a florist and nurseryman in old New York: "I have reason to thank the gods for his diligence, which enabled me to finish my professional training without having to earn my own living" (Washburn 1932:333). Several families, including Washburn's, had both the means to travel to Europe during the daughter's adolescence and the desire to offer this kind of cultural enrichment to their children.

The "family claim," representing the ties and obligations of daughters to family, was an important element in the lives of these women. It asserted itself forcefully during the college careers of two women who were required to interrupt their studies and return home to assist the family in caring for younger siblings who were ill. Devotion and closeness to the mother was especially compelling in the lives of several of these women. We have already described this attachment in the case of Calkins and Shinn (in chapters 1 and 2), but it is evident also in Washburn (see chapter 4) and several of the others. It is worth noting that none of these women married. In each case, the daughter assumed a strongly protective stance toward her mother in adulthood, and for at least two, the mother demonstrated unusual pride and satisfaction in the daughter and her work.

Solomon has noted the importance of maternal encouragement for daughters pursuing collegiate interests and suggests that "a mother's support might relate to her own difficult life or thwarted ambitions" (1985:68). This might well have been true in Washburn's case, for a lifetime acquaintance of hers commented:

Her love for her mother was the strongest emotion of her life. She told me repeatedly that her mother was a perfect human being—that she had never seen a fault in her. And her mother, who loved her and was quietly proud of her achievement, once told me that she considered her less her daughter than her contribution to the race. (Macurdy 1940:5)

Another woman who was unusually devoted to her mother was Naomi Norsworthy (see appendix A for a cameo of Norsworthy). The strong attachment is described in a biography published shortly after Norsworthy's death by a friend who knew both mother and daughter and had opportunity to interview people who had known Norsworthy from childhood (Higgins 1918). The following passage is but one indication of the mutual admiration and companionship shared by this pair:

"Mother and I are such good chums," Miss Norsworthy would say. She made it a rule to share intimately with her mother all her concerns and interests, for the sake of counsel as well as comradeship. Till the close of her own life she bore in mind her mother's wishes; long after most people would have abandoned the maternal ideas as guides for immaturity only, she had her pleasure in deferring to them. . . . She felt she could never render to her mother any part of all she owed her, and deference to her least wish was but slight tribute. (Higgins 1918:38)

Naomi Norsworthy died when she was forty, shortly after her mother. In a sense, her entire life was dominated by the strong values her mother instilled in her, but there is no hint of resentment on the daughter's part.

EDUCATION

The importance of a high status occupation was a prominent feature of American society in the late nineteenth century. One observer commented on this in 1895:

Naomi Norsworthy (1877–1916). (Reprinted from F. C. Higgins, The Life of Naomi Norsworthy *(1918).)*

In a country where there is no titled class, no landed class, no military class, the chief distinction which popular sentiment can lay hold of as raising one set of persons above another is the character of their occupation, the degree of culture it implies, the extent to which it gives them an honourable prominence. (James Bryce cited in Bledstein 1976:34)

As a stepping stone to occupational status, the academic degree was also highly prized. Increasingly "the school diploma . . . served as the license [for] entry into the respectability and rewards of a profession." For the American middle class, education became "an instrument of ambition and a vehicle to status in the occupational world" (Bledstein 1976:33 and 34). The value placed on higher education helps explain the push for collegiate training of women that came in the later decades of the nineteenth century, the sacrifices families were willing to make for ambitious daughters, and the persistence of the women themselves.

All of the early women psychologists were college trained, though not all received bachelor's degrees.[6] Those who earned the baccalaureate did so between the years 1869 and 1903. The extremes in age at time of college graduation ranged from eighteen to thirty–one. Most were in their early twenties when they completed undergraduate study despite the fact that about a third of the women delayed college entrance, spending the intervening years between secondary and higher education as teachers in public and private schools. Presumably, these women worked to support themselves and acquire funds for college, though for some the desire for collegiate training may have developed only during their teaching years. Two women found it necessary to leave college for an interim because of financial pressures, and one "worked her way through college" by simultaneously serving on the faculty of that college.

More than half of the women earned their undergraduate degrees from private women's colleges in the Northeast. Only one woman educated in this region took her degree at a private coeducational institution. The remainder studied at coeducational schools outside of the Northeast, most completing their degrees in newly established state universities and a few in private institutions.[7] Generally women in the Northeast were limited to women's colleges because there were fewer opportunities for coeducation in that part of the country. The majority of schools outside of this region were publicly supported and moved more rapidly to accepting women and men on an equal basis, though not without great controversy (Solomon 1985).

Close proximity to home and family was apparently an important factor in the choice of college for most of these women. The majority attended colleges in their hometowns or at a nearby location. Several lived at home rather than at school. The financial strain that college costs placed on families of "middling" means probably accounted for a woman's remaining nearby or even at home. Family ties were another factor. One woman offered this as her reason, reflecting on her father's insistence that she attend Wellesley: "You felt so sure he cared about you and what you wanted to do that you did not mind when he set limits to your freedom, as when he insisted I should go to a college where I could come home every week-end on Mother's account" (Memories of My Father John Louis Rousmaniere, FRDP).

All but one of the women pursued graduate study. Most received the Ph.D. Some had earned but were denied the degree because of their gender, as was true for Calkins and Ladd-Franklin. Only one woman did not complete her program; marriage, illness, and childbirth came during the year she was preparing for her final examination, which she failed.

Women psychologists at the doctoral level, unlike the men, were severely limited in their opportunities for graduate study because of the discriminatory policies of many institutions. Men had a much wider choice of places to study. The nineteen women with Ph.D.s in our group received them between 1894 and 1906 from nine institutions.[8] The male membership of the APA in 1907, in contrast, had received degrees from as many as twenty-eight institutions, many of which had excluded women.[9] Futhermore, the women APA members received their degrees somewhat later than the men, probably because of entrance restrictions on women as well as their later recognition of psychology as a possible field of study.

The journey from college to graduate study was not a direct one for most of these women. Indeed, a straight path to the advanced degree was not typical for either men or women. Nine of the women in our group (significantly, the younger ones) did go on without interruption. Two married shortly after college graduation but soon returned to do graduate work. The twelve who did not go directly from college to graduate study all held teaching positions, in secondary and normal schools and at women's colleges.

Several factors were operating to delay their entry into doctoral work. For those who wanted to continue their education but were self-supporting, it was necessary to find a paying job for a time. Others may have been daunted by questions such as where to go or how to get admitted. Also, it is likely that few considered psychology as a field for themselves at the time of college graduation. It was not at all clear what a woman could do with a doctoral degree, and families may have resisted further education, seeing this as making a daughter less marriageable. Probably many of the women hesitated to commit themselves to a career, which might threaten their possibilities of marriage and motherhood.[10]

The reasons why they chose psychology as a field for doctoral study are known for only some of the women. In previous chapters we have already described the quite varied circumstances attracting a few of them. Calkins was asked to teach psychology at Wellesley while she was a member of the Greek Department there. Ladd-Franklin was interested in mathematical problems and, while examining the nature of binocular vision, was led to work being done in Germany on visual sensation and perception. Washburn found psychology compelling because it appeared to combine her strong intellectual interests in science and philosophy. Shinn began doctoral work in psychology as a result of positive reactions to her baby study; her entrance into the field seems not to have been planned or associated with any expectation of becoming "a psychologist."

Naomi Norsworthy appears to have been the only woman in our group who was actively recruited by a mentor. After reading the first paper Norsworthy wrote for her beginning psychology course at Teachers College, E.L. Thorndike, the head of the department, asked her to stay after class and complimented her on the work. Until then, she had been planning to become a teacher of chemistry, but "from that day her subject for specialization became psychology" (Higgins 1918:68). Another woman who had an unusual entry into psychology was Lillien Jane Martin, whose cameo is presented in appendix A.

Several of the women continued their formal education in psychology even after completing doctoral study. During the first decade of the twentieth century, eight of them traveled to Europe to study in laboratories where many psychologists had taken their degrees. Berlin was the favorite site, but the American women also worked at Göttingen, Würzburg, Leipzig, and Heidelberg.

LIFE-STYLES

Whether or not they had definite professional ambitions, these women began doctoral study with a strong intrinsic motivation to explore psychology as an intellectual endeavor. It is likely that many did not know how they might use their training: graduate study did not necessarily signify a career commitment. Subsequently their lives developed in a variety of ways. Several of them met a marriage partner while in graduate school; some of these made no effort to pursue a career whereas some who married did manage later to combine marriage and career. Others remained single and made a lifetime commitment to a career, in psychology or an ancillary field.

While they broke with convention by pursuing advanced education and careers, these women nevertheless adopted

Lillien Jane Martin (1851–1943). (Reprinted from M. A. deFord, Psychologist Unretired: The Life of Lillien J. Martin *(1948).)*

manners that were largely congruent with their upbringing. Though by entering a professional field they were challenging the accepted social order, they did not flaunt their difference from other women, nor did they challenge conventions in an audacious way. Rather, they tended to adhere to the widely accepted code of prudent and genteel behavior expected of women of their day and class. Generally theirs was a quiet, private rebellion against the restrictions of women's sphere and its emphasis on domesticity.

One of the women, however, did specifically confront the issue of women's sphere. Early in the century in an address dealing with education, Kate Gordon wrote:

The question of woman's education is seductively close to the question of woman's "sphere." I hold it to be almost a transgression even to mention woman's sphere—the word recalls so many painful and impertinent deliveries, so much of futile discussion about it—and yet the willingness to dogmatize about woman in general is so common an infirmity that I am emboldened to err. (Gordon 1905:789)

Though several women in our group wrote on the topic of women's education, there is little evidence in their scholarly work that they actively questioned widely held conceptions of the female role. Ethel Puffer, as we have shown in chapter 3, labored to broaden women's role to include intellectual and professional dimensions, but still held to the belief that maternity and domesticity were central in the lives of women. Helen Thompson's psychological research may be seen as the most significant confrontation of social mores produced by any of these women. In her doctoral thesis, Thompson (1903) called into serious question common cultural assumptions about the inferiority of women and the presumed biological basis of "female" characteristics—notions that had been used to justify confining women's activity to the domestic realm. (See appendix A for a cameo of Thompson.)

Several of the women—including especially Christine Ladd-Franklin, Lillien Martin, and Helen Thompson—actively supported women's suffrage. Generally, they did so by calmly

Helen Bradford Thompson (1874–1947). (Courtesy of Eleanor Fowler.)

presenting reasoned arguments; outrageous behavior was alien to them. Others, however, seemed simply to ignore the calls for support of suffrage, and some were even uncomfortable with the term "feminist." None of them played such a significant role as to figure prominently in a history of the suffrage movement. Nor did any of these women seek a radical reform of the general social order as did some women of their age.[11] Ladd-Franklin was the most outspoken on women's rights, but her efforts were directed mainly toward gaining educational equality for women through admission to graduate schools. She was active in promoting the work of the Association of Collegiate Alumnae (the forerunner of the American Association of University Women), and a few of the other women psychologists benefited from the ACA fellowship program and worked to support ACA's advancement.

These women best demonstrated their pioneering spirits by pursuing and earning advanced degrees. Some of them were content to stop after earning the Ph.D., while others continued in academic careers to the extent they could. Several entered careers only tangentially related to their specific training, and in those contexts a few participated in projects typical of progressive reforms. These last were the women who moved into applied fields, as discussed in our next chapter.

Joyce Antler (1980), whose work we cited in chapter 2, studied the Wellesley College graduates in the class of 1897 (a group quite similar in backgrounds to the women in our work) and found that postcollegiate women could be categorized into five groups: ladies of leisure, working daughters, queen mothers, experimenters, and independents. She described their life-styles on the basis of residence (in parental home, marital home, or neither) and employment. Many of the 1897 Wellesley graduates returned to the family home after graduation and combined care for parents with such things as club work, church activities, and visiting (Antler's "ladies of leisure"). Others who returned home also took up a paid vocation, most often teaching, becoming "working daughters." Of those who did not live in parental homes, most were married: the "queen mothers," who typically moved from college back to parental home and then to marital home as wives; and the "experimenters," who spent some time before marriage employed in a traditionally feminine occupation (e.g. teaching or social work). Only a very few of the Wellesley graduates could be considered "independents," unmarried career women living alone or with other women. Note that for her group, Antler did not need a term to identify *married* women having a career, as this was such a rare combination.

Residence, marital status, and type of work are indeed significant factors shaping the experiences of women. Applying Antler's classification to the women psychologists highlights how the experience of professional women was different from the adult life-styles chosen by their sister college graduates. We follow Antler's scheme to show that our group of psychologists was a select subset of turn-of-the-century women and to give an indication of how their lives were organized in adulthood.

First it should be noted that none of the women psychologists properly falls into the categories of "ladies of leisure" or "queen mothers," for all of them engaged in paid employment at some time following college graduation. This combined with their pursuit of advanced degrees demonstrates a high degree of independence during young adulthood for all of our group. Only three of the psychologists were "working daughters," living at home and carrying responsibilities for parents as well teaching in higher education.

Nearly half of our group (11) could be called "independents." They all pursued teaching careers at the postsecondary level after receiving the doctorate. Within this group, moreover, seven may be considered highly independent in that they worked in settings unusual for women and experienced a number of job and location changes. Six of these taught in coeducational institutions at some time, and two of them eventually married late in life. Five among the "independents" finally settled into the way of life most typical of academic women: teaching at a women's college, the most frequent occupational listing for first-generation women psychologists.

Three of these held appointments at Wellesley College, as did one of the "working daughters" mentioned above.

The living conditions experienced by these women at Wellesley have been described in detail by Palmieri (1983). They lived and worked in an especially supportive environment, one that was called an "Adamless Eden" and "a little world under one roof." A strong sense of community and commitment to common goals and interests prevailed:

Wellesley was very much like an extended family. Its members, with shared backgrounds and tastes, shared visions of life and work, and often shared bonds of family or prior friendship, could hardly but produce an extraordinary community. In this milieu, no one was isolated, no one forgotten. . . . Individual patterns of association overlapped: one's friends were also friends and colleagues to each other. Networks which provided both social camaraderie and intellectual stimulation were characteristic of the Wellesley community. . . . faculty were not merely professional associates but astonishingly good friends. They formed a world whose symbols were respect for learning, love of nature, devotion to social activism, a fondness for wit and humor, frequent emotional exchanges, and loyalty to Wellesley and to each other. (Palmieri 1983:203)

In this professional and social context, collaboration was standard and women served as mentors and role models to each other. Mothers and sisters of faculty members were frequently part of the community as well. For example, the sister of Anna McKeag, one of the women psychologists at Wellesley, kept house for her, relieved her of many domestic duties, and was a beloved member of the Wellesley scene. Thus the women enjoyed an environment that supported their commitment to scholarship and at the same time nourished their personal development, despite the reality of limitations placed on their advancement in the discipline (see discussions in chapters 4 and 7).

Wellesley was unique among the women's colleges in its all-women faculty, and each of the women's colleges had distinct features affecting faculty life, but the possibilities for stable careers and long-term friendships with like-minded women favored the personal situation of those women who settled into the pattern of single women academics at women's colleges.[12]

More than a third of our subjects were "experimenters" by Antler's definition, women who married, but after a period of professional employment. Most of them met their husbands while both were students, so it is not suprising that almost all of the husbands of these women followed academic careers, several of them in psychology. These women, then, shared their lives with men who had congruent educational backgrounds and experienced social settings that supported their own intellectual and cultural interests. For them, however, there were pressing demands unrelated to their academic training, tied to the roles of wife, mother, and housekeeper. Almost all of them returned to professional work after a period of childrearing, and seven of the nine experimenters were in paid employment positions for most of their adult lives. They managed to accomplish this by taking unusual assignments and effectively building them into substantial and ongoing projects. They created their own opportunities for advancement depending on the conditions presented by family needs and changes in location required by family moves. Their creativity often involved operating outside both the traditional boundaries of academic psychology and those assigned to women. For this reason, it is necessary to distinguish them even from Antler's venturesome independents and experimenters. We call them "adapters." This group, who sought to enlarge a woman's opportunities by combining family and career, modeled a life-style later generations of women psychologists tended to follow in greater numbers.

The early women psychologists, then, exhibit two predominant postdoctoral life patterns, differentiated by their marital status. The women who remained single generally were able to pursue uninterrupted careers, most of them in personally satisfying settings committed to women's education. Women who chose to marry disqualified themselves from academic employment and changed locations as required by the spouse's work, but some nevertheless managed to find innovative ways of carving out meaningful careers.

Our sample of women who entered an emerging scientific field is quite different from Antler's college graduates. Their life experiences shed some light on what historians Joan Jacobs Brumberg and Nancy Tomes identify as "a crucial element in the modern evolution of the professions: the entry of middle-class women into the professional milieu" (1982:275). The women who obtained advanced training in psychology demonstrated an overwhelming drive to continue in careers. Whereas their entry into graduate programs may have been motivated by several factors—economic need for self and family support, family expectations and encouragement, occupational mobility, intellectual fascination with the subject— these women emerged with a strong urge to persevere, to use their skills in various ways dependent on their individual circumstances. Career-related activities became important for personal fulfillment. This was especially true for the high proportion of women who married. They did not have to work for economic reasons, and working outside the home required making troublesome accommodations in family life. That they did so suggests a dedication arising from both their individual experiences and the social ethic in which they had been reared. Their advanced education had opened new vistas to them and apparently in their eyes also carried a responsibility for putting their training to good use.

CHAPTER 7

Careers and Contributions

Career and life-style are intimately related. Each presents opportunities and limitations that impinge on the other. To a great extent, career choice is a good predictor of adult life-style because it influences such things as geographical location, how and where time is spent, social encounters and relationships, amount of income and how income is used—all integral elements of one's life-style. And likewise, certain life-style choices have profound effects on career possibilities. For example, a woman's decisions concerning marriage and motherhood may open doors to certain careers while at the same time making others impossible, just as a decision to undertake a career may enhance or interfere with certain marriage and parenting possibilities. Speaking of career in terms of choices introduces an important component: commitment. When we consider the careers of women psychologists, we are referring to the commitments made by these women to spend their lives in particular settings, engaged in certain kinds of activities.

The issue of career development is a complicated one for the group we are describing, partially because of the variety of patterns seen in the women's lives and partially because of confusion in the use of terms such as career, vocation, work, and profession. Here we use "career" to refer to active, long-term involvement in specialized work, e.g., psychology as a profession. Such involvement may or may not coincide with employment as paid work. Similarly, either career or employment may or may not confer professional status, as that term implies recognition for particular achievements in training and practice in a given field. Thus among the first generation of women psychologists we find some who pursued lifelong careers, combined with steady employment and professional status, in psychology or in a related field. Others pursued careers and even gained professional status although they were not regularly employed. And then there were those who did not pursue a professional career after having received the prerequisite training.

The question of how to use one's education once finished with doctoral study may have caused even greater concern among our subjects than the after-college identity crisis often experienced by late nineteenth-century women (see discussion in chapter 2). Graduate study differentiated the psychologists even more from typical middle-class women. Their situation was complicated by the lack of role models and the attitudes of the men who directed their graduate work. Though several of the women received enthusiastic support from mentors, many psychologists probably shared the sentiments of Carl Seashore (dean of the Graduate College of the University of Iowa from 1908 to 1936 and professionally prominent in both psychology and education), who "early on . . . concluded that women who pursued graduate work were abnormal" (Jones 1978:171).

Seashore argued that *graduate* education for women had its chief value in preparing them to be cultivated wives for professional men and believed that the normal woman "pursued marriage and family first, and education only as an aid to sustaining and inspiring the married state" (Jones 1978:174). He deplored the "career woman," who was likely to be "mannish" and in danger of becoming a "neurotic old maid," but paradoxically believed that preparation for a career—to be pursued during the premarriage period—was important. He and his wife, a graduate in philosophy, agreed that for women marriage is a career in itself, with fine children being greater assets and sources of satisfaction than many professional products. From Seashore's perspective, "when a brilliant and attractive woman receives her Doctor's degree there is usually a young man around the corner" (Seashore 1942:239–40).

To what extent did the early women psychologists meet Seashore's expectations? Though they may not have had definite career goals when they were in graduate school, all but two of them held professional employment at some time following advanced study—and one of those was Milicent Shinn, who did continue some professional work in child study, though unemployed. Despite considerable variety in the career and employment histories of these twenty-five women, three distinct patterns emerge to categorize their postdoctoral activities: teaching (mainly at women's colleges), applied work, and homemaking (both with and without sporadic employment). By 1920 these patterns become clear ways of grouping the women. Their situations are not easily differentiated earlier because, though several had met future husbands during their graduate school days (as Seashore would have predicted), all but four followed graduate study with academic employment and all who married were devoted to homemaking during the childrearing years.[1]

TEACHING

Among the women who "went to work" after advanced study, all took teaching positions—and all but one at the postsecondary level. Several continued as instructors at the institutions where they had been graduate students or returned to the institutions they had left in order to pursue the doctorate.

The importance of teaching as a career opportunity for these women is highlighted in the statement one of them made when comparing her own generation to that of the "modern girl" in 1929: "Most of us in our time meant to teach and said so" (Gamble 1929:8). Teaching was, after all, the only professional role for which women's higher education was distinctly preparatory. It was *the* profession for career-minded women in the nineteenth century. As discussed in chapter 6, many had taught before doing graduate work. Advanced degrees, however, qualified psychologists to teach at higher levels in the educational system. Because these were women, however, upward occupational mobility was not assured them. First, there was the stricture against women instructing men. Educated women were concentrated in teaching, and as they began to predominate as teachers at the lower levels there was a growing alarm over the feminization of the schools, specifically focusing on dangers to the masculinity of boys subjected to instruction by women. This alarm provoked strong resistance to women's entry as teachers of young men at the college and university level. And second, there was a prohibition against a *married* woman teaching anyone—other than her own children. Even at the women's colleges, marriage meant that a woman faculty member lost her position.

Immediately following doctoral study, the majority of the women (13) were employed as faculty at women's colleges. Four held positions at normal schools, which granted teacher preparation degrees rather than baccalaureates. Only three women joined faculties of four-year coeducational institutions.

Some experiences of the women who held long-term appointments at coeducational schools illustrate the particular difficulties they faced in male-dominated situations: slow advancement in academic rank and difficulty in demonstrating competence. Mabel Clare Williams was the first woman as well as the first psychologist to receive a Ph.D. from the University of Iowa. Despite her Ph.D., she was kept at the instructor level for four years and was assistant professor for ten (1910–1920), whereas a younger man with a newly received Ph.D. was recruited into the department at the associate level in 1914. After eighteen years on the faculty at Iowa, still not promoted to full professor, Williams resigned in 1924 to marry a former classmate. During this time, Seashore, who was Williams' department head and whose courses she "assisted," argued against granting scholarship money to women pursuing graduate work on the basis of a study showing that in a matched sample of stipend holders from his Graduate College, surveyed five or more years after graduation, forty or more men had become leaders in their fields, filling positions such as presidents and deans, whereas the highest academic

Kate Gordon (1878–1963). (Courtesy of the University Archives, Department of Special Collections, University of California, Los Angeles.)

achievement of a woman was assistant professor (Jones 1978). Presumably that woman was Williams, whose career he himself may have thwarted.

Kate Gordon and Naomi Norsworthy also taught at coeducational institutions. Gordon, whose cameo is in appendix A, held the longest tenure and is distinguished by the number and wide scope of her scholarly publications. Her advancement in rank, however, was slow and erratic, and only by chance did she become head of the department at the University of California at Los Angeles for a short time. Naomi Norsworthy's experiences at Columbia's Teachers College reveal a different problem: the personal challenges facing a woman instructor of men. By becoming an exemplary professor at a coeducational institution, Norsworthy was no longer identified as a woman and became a "strong man" (see cameo in appendix A).

Women faculty at the women's colleges, on the other hand, lived and worked in a setting that was supportive of career development at the local level and a welcome haven for those who found a permanent place there. Five of the women who were first employed at women's colleges resigned within a few years to marry (as did one woman at a normal school). Two shifted from a single-sex college to a coeducational institution, but for one of those that was only a short foray, as she returned to women's education after only three years. Therefore, six of the women (all unmarried) spent almost their entire postdoctoral careers at a women's college, while two others (likewise unmarried) were also primarily engaged in women's education though at normal schools.

The advantages of teaching at a women's college were that women faculty were more likely to be viewed as competent by colleagues and students, less likely to be competing with men, and therefore better able to advance than women at co-educational institutions. In this special atmosphere, they moved smoothly through the academic ranks, often enjoying positions of prestige and status on their own campuses. At the same time, however, their location was a hindrance to full professional advancement because they were disadvantaged in the realm of peer recognition and standing in their discipline.

Women's colleges, as described in chapters 4 and 6, provided less than ideal circumstances for nurturing a career in the sciences, and this was even more true of the normal schools. The faculties were small, and there was little oppportunity for exchange with colleagues in one's own discipline who could provide helpful criticism as well as direct stimulation. Facilities for conducting research were meager. For example, the women's colleges did not have the range or quality of apparatus that existed in the larger laboratories.[2] If experimental work was done at a women's college, it was subject to definite limitations compared with what was available in the research-focused universities—all of which were male-dominated. Furthermore, the primary responsibility was teaching, and heavy teaching loads made excessive demands on time and energy. In these ways, a faculty member at a women's college, despite her socially supportive environment, lacked the research support and exposure to the wider community of scholars that were available to faculty at the universities. Given these circumstances, it is not surprising that, of the eight women at women's colleges and normal schools, only Margaret Washburn at Vassar and Eleanor Gamble at Wellesley continued to contribute to the experimental research literature of psychology.

A further professional handicap was the low prestige associated with being at a women's college. In correspondence between men psychologists, it is clear that the women's colleges were places to be avoided, if possible, by the ambitious man. Titchener, writing to a man about job prospects, mentioned almost as an aside: "There is also a minor place at Randolph Macon Woman's College, Lynchburg, Va., but I don't suppose you'd care for that; lots of teaching and no chance of research" (to [Paul T.] Young, May 24, 1919, EBTP). To another Titchener commented: "You are right in general about the handicap of a woman's college but Wellesley is a good place to get out from, and it won't hurt you to have even as long as ten years in your present environment. Ultimately I imagine you will pass on to some state university" (to M. J. Zigler, January 7, 1925, EBTP). We have already noted (in chapter 4) that Noble MacCracken, when president at Vassar College, did not expect to keep his "creative" men faculty—they were "likely to leave soon." He himself had been told by a frank colleague when he was considering a move from the Yale faculty: "You are throwing your life away to go off and teach girls at Smith College" (MacCracken 1950:1). It was widely understood that wherever women are found, that place is lesser.

APPLIED WORK

At the time the first women entered the field, psychologists found employment only in academic settings. Even then it was becoming apparent, however, that psychologists in America might have much to offer in real-life settings, outside the psychological laboratory and the traditional classroom of the ivied campuses. As scientific psychology migrated across the Atlantic, brought to America by those who had studied in the European laboratories, it changed, responding to American zeal for practicality. And as psychology began to "come of age," it did so during a period of general social change. In 1913 Woodrow Wilson articulated a widespread optimism: "This is nothing short of a new social age, a new era of human relationships, a new stage-setting for the drama of life" (cited in Morison 1965:812). Not suprisingly, many psychologists believed that they could participate in bringing about the "perfectability of man."[3] Their involvement in such efforts as the mental health movement, the child study movement, the development of mental tests, and the rise of educational psychology demonstrated that psychologists believed they had a mission that went beyond the disinterested collection of basic data and theory building.

Thus psychologists began to develop, alongside academic psychology, the diverse area of applied psychology. We are using the term "applied" to refer to the use of psychological principles and discoveries for practical ends. For example, work in child psychology may be either basic (i.e., designed to extend knowledge about children through research) or applied (designed to discover means of advancing child welfare or of providing services for children based on what is known about child development). Applied work may involve research as well as delivery of professional services, but the goal in either case is utilitarian rather than theoretical. As we use the terms, both academic and applied psychology are subsumed under "professional psychology."

Several of the first-generation women psychologists moved into applied areas after having begun as academics. For four of them, the switch in careers was necessitated by marriage. Each of these married women returned to professional work after several years of housekeeping and childrearing, and each was then compelled to find work in applied settings, which changed as the husband's career took them to different locations. The situations of Ethel Puffer and Helen Thompson are described in chapter 3 and appendix A. Eleanor Rowland and Jessie Allen also left faculty positions when they married. Rowland eventually gained international reputation through writing and lecturing to a wide audience on her work in correctional psychology during the 1920s and 1930s. Significantly, her statement of research interests, as listed in *AMS,* was changed in this period to read "psychology for the lay public." Allen was for a time a research fellow and then a consulting psychologist (an "applied" title) at several academic institutions before becoming chair of adult education at Ohio State University where she published and lectured frequently on parent education. Her husband was a prominent educator, and two of their four children earned doctoral degrees in psychology.[4]

Three of the unmarried women also worked in applied psychology. Margaret Smith's efforts in this area appear to have been a limited engagement. Most of her career was spent educating teachers in the New York normal schools at Oswego and New Paltz. Her academic work was interrupted, however, between 1909 and 1918 when she reported as her employment "supervisor of education of a family." Subsequently she added "retarded development of a child" as an area of research interest in her *AMS* listing.

Elizabeth Adams, after taking her Ph.D., spent nine years at Smith College where she instituted the department of education. She resigned in 1916 because of prolonged illness. During World War I she returned to work in the professional section of the U.S. War Emergency Employment Service. From that experience she concluded that the greatest benefit college women gained from their war experiences was a sense of competence as professionals. Adams published *Women Professional Workers* (1921), an influential book that provided a comprehensive survey of occupational possibilities for women and signified her shift to the field of vocational guidance. During the 1920s and 1930s, she was educational secretary of Girl Scouts, Inc.[5]

Theodate Smith's applied interests and activity were in the area of child welfare and development. Hers is the career that comes closest to approximating the subordinate "women's work" described by Margaret Rossiter (1982) and discussed later in this chapter. Smith's cameo is included in appendix A.

In summary, many of the women psychologists had careers first in academic and then in applied psychology. Lillien Martin provides the most dramatic example of the sequential career pattern, as shown in her cameo in appendix A. The shift of some of the early women from academic to applied psychology foreshadowed the gender segregation that developed when women began to find employment more readily in applied areas (see chapter 8).

HOMEMAKING

About half (12) of the twenty-five women married at some time. This is a high marriage rate for women Ph.D.s, another fact that marks these women as unusual, for "75 per cent of the women who earned Ph.D.s [in all fields] between 1877 and 1924 remained spinsters" (Chafe 1972:100). All of those who married had children except for the one woman who was widowed within a year of marriage and the two who married late in life. Most of them resisted the finality of the marriage-career dichotomy and found employment outside the home for a significant portion of their lives. Only three (Hamlin, Bagley, and Rousmaniere) made a career of marriage. Thus a mere 12 per-

Theodate L. Smith (1859–1914). (Courtesy of the Smith College Archives.)

cent of this group met Seashore's expectations for how a woman graduate student would choose to use her training.

Alice Hamlin and Florence Winger Bagley, both students of E. B. Titchener, married fellow students in the doctoral program at Cornell. Hamlin received her Ph.D. in 1896, then taught as professor of psychology at Mt. Holyoke College for a year before marrying and moving to Nebraska where her husband, Edgar L. Hinman, was teaching philosophy. There she was an assistant instructor in psychology for two years prior to the birth of her daughter. The family continued to live in Lincoln, where she was quite active in community and church organizations, as well as occasionally lecturing in teachers' institutes and at the University of Nebraska School of Nursing (between 1928 and 1932).

Florence Bagley married in 1901. Her husband had completed his degree the year before and taken a position in the West. In the year she remained at Cornell, Florence completed her thesis research but did not take her oral examination before leaving for her wedding in the summer. During the next year, she suffered a long illness with remittant malarial fever and gave birth to a daughter in May of 1902. The following September her husband wrote to her adviser concerning her examination which had taken place that summer and her acute disappointment at having failed. He felt that the circumstances under which she had been placed had had a severely detrimental effect and indicated that she planned to attempt the examination again at a later date. He also expressed hope that she would be able to obtain her degree and his willingness to aid her, along with his assurance that if she did not complete the requirements for her degree they would reimburse the university for the amount of her scholarships and fellowship. He acknowledged, however, that "at present domestic duties engross her attention exclusively, and it will be two years, at the very least, before a new beginning could be made" (W. C. Bagley to E. B. Titchener, September 1, 1902, EBTP). Eleven months later, however, Florence Bagley gave birth to her second son—and domestic duties continued to engross her as two more children were born. The family made several moves about the country while her husband pursued a highly successful career as a nationally recognized educator.

The best glimpse into the experience of a married woman is provided by the papers of Frances H. Rousmaniere. These are excerpted in her cameo in appendix A. A thoughtful woman,

Frances Rousmaniere (1876–1964). (Courtesy of the Wellesley College Archives.)

she recorded many of her ideas, and both her journal notes and the regular letters written to her Wellesley classmates trace her efforts to accommodate to the demands of modern family life.

For the fiftieth anniversary of her 1898 Wellesley class, when she was in her seventies, Rousmaniere wrote:

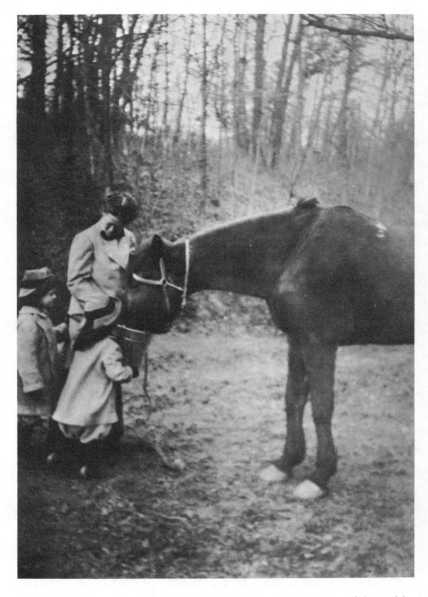

Frances Rousmaniere Dewing and Children. (Courtesy of the Schlesinger Library, Radcliffe College.)

I have taught calculus at Bennington College and become interested in physics for the first time during these last five years. . . . I think at the moment housekeeping and grandmothering are my activities and reading of current events and semi-popular science my hobbies, with interest in some modern painting thrown in. . . . The most important things in life seem to me to be: an awareness of the marvel of things little and big all about us, both in human beings and in Nature; an alertness to learn and to do whatever we can that shall make possible such awareness in others, as well as in ourselves. (Record of Class of '98, Fiftieth Anniversary, 1898–1948:76, WCA)

Rousmaniere also indicates that her education, never intended to be professional training, stirred serious interests that remained dominant and enriched her life, though she did not follow a professional career. Husband, children, and housekeeping were central in her activities. Her daughters, two of whom received master's degrees, believe that she lived a highly satisfying life.

CONTRIBUTIONS

Among the psychologists in our study were women widely recognized by their peers for important contributions to the new discipline. By the time the third edition of *American Men of Science* appeared in 1921, six of the women had received stars in their listing: Calkins, Ladd-Franklin, and Washburn in the 1906 edition; Martin and Puffer in 1910; and Thompson in 1921. Stars indicated eminence in the field and were based on a confidential peer rating system devised by James McKeen Cattell. In 1903 about a fourth of those listed in each of the sciences were designated as being among the top 1000 scientists in the country; these received stars in the 1906 *AMS* for distinction in research. In psychology the first three women (who ranked twelfth, nineteenth, and forty-second out of fifty) represented 6 percent of the starred psychologists in 1903, when women constituted 6.7 percent of the field based on APA membership.[6]

Margaret Rossiter (1982: ch. 3), in her comprehensive study of women in American science, has shown that nineteenth-century science typically segregated women by confining them to "women's work"—either tedious, low-status tasks (hierarchical segregation) or limited subareas of a field (territorial segregation). We do not find this phenomenon operating for the early women psychologists. They were exposed to the full spectrum of content areas defining the psychology of their time and made substantive contributions in a wide range of topics.

An article assessing the status of American psychology in 1904 (Miner) noted that already the field had become differentiated in its subject matter. The most prominent subfields then were educational psychology and comparative psychology. In addition to the regular descriptive and experimental psychology, courses were being taught on a wide variety of other topics. A later review discussed new areas of interest that developed between 1892 and 1917 (Pillsbury 1917).[7] It is worth emphasizing that, with the exception of experimental phonetics, each of these subareas was represented in the work of early women, indicating their involvement in all areas of the discipline. In fact, the women engaged in teaching and research in areas that spanned the breadth of the discipline in a pattern not discernibly different from the men, for men too were working in all of these areas. The most notable difference between men and women psychologists is that women were less likely to be working. When they were employed, they were more likely to be teaching than doing research, though men still held most of the teaching positions (Boring 1920, Fernberger 1928).

Although there appears to have been no special "women's work" for these psychologists, in the sense of exclusive hierarchical tasks or content areas, there was a definite "women's place." The women were employed for the most part in educational institutions where they were primarily expected to teach psychology rather than add to its research base. This situation applies to the men as well; it is significant, however, that the women were concentrated in a certain kind of teaching environment, that which provided higher education for women—the women's colleges or normal schools. With their employment restricted to that type of academic setting, women were faced with several obstacles against their full development as participants in the new science.

Earlier in the chapter we discussed several of these limitations, including lack of support for research and the low status of women's colleges. Futhermore, academic positions were limited in number at the women's colleges and normal schools. Those who sought academic employment were hard pressed to find work as psychologists, for once psychology was added to the curriculum of an institution those employed were likely to stay put until retirement. And men, too, were competing for teaching posts in the women's colleges and normal schools, though highly qualified men may have been discouraged from doing so because of the very limitations the women were forced to tolerate. Then there was also the prohibition against married women as faculty, making academic careers at any institution impossible for women after marriage.[8]

PUBLICATIONS

Despite these many obstacles, the first-generation women were remarkably productive. A tabulation of author entries in a cumulative index of psychological writings from 1894 to 1958, which encompasses almost the entire period of these women's careers, gives a total of 411 publications for the twenty-five women.[9] The number of publications per woman ranged from 0 to 83, with an average of 16; half the women published 8 or more items and half, 5 or fewer. By comparison, an equal number of men randomly selected from the APA membership in 1907 had a range of 0 to 100 publications, with an average of 26 and half of the men publishing 17 or more. It is surprising that the disparity of publication rates is not greater given the women's exclusion from academic positions and supportive scientific networks.

The topics on which the women wrote cover the full range of content and methodology in psychology. The earlier works tend to be based on doctoral thesis research, including such topics as the sensation of pain, aesthetics, rhythm and work, mental development of children, and even the psychology of the guinea pig. Later in their careers, as the women's interests and professional needs evolved, the nature of their contributions changed. Only a few continued to publish experimental work, probably because of women's lack of access to necessary apparatus and assistants. A number of the women published regular literature reviews of various areas. They also contributed general discussion papers as well as theoretical works, technical reports, and writings that interpreted psychology to the lay public.

The influence of works published by the women early in their careers may be assessed in part by examining a series of reports on "progress in psychology" spanning the years 1903 to 1912. The reports charted changes in the focus of the discipline, the growth of psychology as indicated by the granting of Ph.D.s, and significant events in the field. In addition, the author of these annual reviews, a starred psychologist in 1903, also selectively mentioned major contributors. Women whose works are highlighted include Martin, Calkins, Washburn, Gordon, and Gamble (in descending order of frequency). The most enthusiastic praise went to Washburn for *The Animal Mind:* "A most interesting, if not, perhaps, the most distinctive, achievement of the year is to be found among the credits of American psychology. Miss Washburn's book performs the special service of giving the first systematic presentation of the recently developed field indicated by its title" (Buchner 1909:1–2).

Titchener also published his evaluation of work done during the first decade of the twentieth century. Though he dealt exclusively with experimental psychology, he mentioned by name the studies of Martin, Thompson, Gordon, M.K. Smith, Gamble, and Calkins. He also included an offhand salute to his former doctoral student Washburn, but without giving her name: "The present status of comparative psychology has already been set forth by an authority far more competent than myself" (Titchener 1910:419).

These commentaries and the *AMS* stars indicate the prominence gained by some of the women psychologists in the eyes of their professional peers. Several of them, moreover, published books that were reviewed for a general audience. The index to *Book Review Digest,* covering 1905 to 1974, lists twenty-five books written by twelve of the women. These are almost equally divided between theoretical works, general and applied subjects, and texts presenting syntheses. The topics treated range over many subjects, though almost three-fourths of the works may be classified as educational psychology, philosophy, aesthetics, guidance, or applied. The most widely reviewed book was Washburn's *The Animal Mind* (1908). Reviews were generally quite positive regarding content and style, whether in psychological journals or lay publications. Several of the reviewers acknowledged the women authors as undisputed authorities in their field, notably Calkins, Ladd-Franklin, and Rowland.

The extent to which scientists are still using the women's work, some of it published more than ninety years ago, is indicated by citations in the current scientific literature. Articles published in scientific journals between 1972 and 1984 cited sixteen of the women for over a hundred of their publications. Washburn, Calkins, and Gordon account for 63 percent of these recent citations of work done by the early women psychologists. This order might be expected, as these three were the women who published most frequently. But it is noteworthy that studies done by others who published very little are still acknowledged in research of present-day psychologists. The most enduring works, i.e., the most heavily cited, are Washburn's *The Animal Mind* (1908), Shinn's *Biography of a Baby* (1900), Calkins' (1896) paper on association of ideas, and Gordon's (1924) experimental study of group judgments of lifted weights.

ORGANIZATIONAL PARTICIPATION

In the nineteenth century, specialized professional associations became a means of establishing and legitimizing a field. The American Psychological Association was organized in 1892 to institutionalize psychology as a distinct discipline. Its object was "the advancement of psychology as a science." Early leaders poured their energy into strengthening the organization, understanding that upon its prestige depended much of their own. Participation in the affairs of the APA became a way of exercising power through the shaping of the new field. It was also an effective way for individuals to build communication networks and gain professional status. The association functioned as a social exchange system, with individuals contributing to the organization for the benefit of the profession and in return receiving public recognition and honor for their efforts.

Though only Calkins and Washburn became prominent in the governance affairs of psychology's professional society, women were readily admitted as members (Goodman 1980c). The association began with a membership of thirty-one men. A council composed of six of the founders was given the responsibility of nominating persons who would then be elected to membership. During the early years, there were no definite qualifications for membership beyond sponsorship by the council; employment status and publications were apparently important considerations, and these were indirectly dependent upon doctoral-level study (Fernberger 1932).[10]

At the APA's second annual meeting, Calkins and Ladd-Franklin were elected along with fourteen men.[11] Apparently these two were sponsored by Cattell, a member of the first council, who wrote to the others asking if they would consent to the women's nomination. In his note to G. S. Fullerton, Cattell added the comment, "I suppose we psychologists ought not to draw a sex-line." To Joseph Jastrow, secretary of the association, he wrote "I wish to propose for membership . . . Mrs. Franklin and Miss Calkins. Please let me know whether you favor the election of these (especially the women), as they may like to attend the meetings if their election is favored by a majority of the Council."[12] Successful in advocating the women, Cattell was able to comment fourteen years later: "We were thus tolerably prompt to recognize equality of opportunity for the sexes, and this record we have maintained, for we now have 39 women among our members" (Cattell 1917:278).

A comprehensive history of the APA published in 1932 discussed the people and events that shaped its evolution during the years when the first generation of psychologists was active (Fernberger 1932). Several women are mentioned in this document, appearing most often in the work of several committees. Committees played a vital function in determining the direction of the profession and regulating its activities. The only woman prominent in this role, however, was Washburn, who not only served on but also chaired two important committees, each of which effectively resolved long-standing problems confronting the APA. Even more significant than committee work, however, was membership on the council, the small group that directed the activities of the organization. Both Calkins and Washburn held the influential council post, Calkins from 1906 to 1908 and Washburn from 1912 to 1914.

Calkins and Washburn were also elected to the office of president. Calkins served in 1905 upon nomination of the council, and Washburn was elected in 1921 by the democratic process of membership nomination and ballot. They were the only women to serve as president of the APA during its first seventy-nine years. Following Washburn, it was to be fifty years—a full half century—before another woman was elected to that honored office.[13]

To summarize, the first generation of women psychologists contributed to the literature of the field in all areas, and their work is still being recognized in ongoing research. Several of them were judged eminent by their peers. They were admitted to APA membership, and two of them held prominent leadership roles in that organization. The careers and contributions of some of the women continued into the midtwentieth century: Jessie Allen (Charters), Kate Gordon (Moore), and Mabel Clare Williams (Kemmerer) were listed in the tenth edition of *American Men of Science* in 1962. Their lives overlapped with women entering the field at later dates. In the next chapter, we briefly sketch the changes in psychology experienced by women who followed the first generation.

CHAPTER 8

To the Present

Many of psychology's first women lived to see important changes taking place in the discipline during the first half of the twentieth century. The most prominent developments were the emergence of applied psychology as a substantial aspect of the field and the sharp schism between academic (scientific) and applied (practical) psychology that came with psychology's successes as a profession.

The applied areas—especially clinical, school, and industrial—gained attention following World War I. Psychologists assisting in the war effort had demonstrated the utility of their practical skills. In the 1920s significant numbers of psychologists extended the range of their activities to include consulting work in applied settings (clinics, schools, businesses, and governmental agencies). Research activities also shifted, so that by the end of the decade nearly half of all psychologists were doing research in applied areas (Fernberger 1928). Professional specialties multiplied, and psychology in its applied form caught the eye of the public. Increasingly, psychologists came to be viewed as experts who could provide advice and assistance in matters of everyday life. Psychologists themselves welcomed the attention and the attribution (Napoli 1981).

Women continued to enter psychology in increasing numbers and proportions relative to men, but they began to be concentrated in the applied subfields. As we noted in chapter 7, there was no clearly demarcated "women's work" in psychology for the first generation of women psychologists, as

tended to be true in the other sciences. However, the movement into applied work that was required of the early married
women (who were excluded from academia) foreshadowed a
segregation based on gender that began to be apparent in the
1920s and accelerated in the 1930s. In 1928, 62 percent of the
women in APA reported fields of research in the applied area
compared with 44 percent in 1920. The changed percentage
reflected a shift of women from experimental work to applied
topics. Over the same period men, too, had increased their
participation in applied research (from 35 percent in 1920 to 43
percent in 1928), but men were still heavily invested in experimental and theoretical work (Fernberger 1928).

The emergence of applied research topics and practical applications presented for both women and men attractive alterna-
tives to the basic scientific work and academic careers that had
characterized psychology around the turn of the century. Influential psychologists (those in control of the APA) insisted
however on retaining the academic, scientific base for psychology. That position was seen as necessary for maintaining the
prestige of the discipline, which psychologists were only recently enjoying vis-à-vis the older and better established
sciences.[1] Applied psychologists early on did not object to this
stance, since they benefited from the fact that their "staging
area" was the university. It gave them greater credibility and
authority as "experts." In competition with other groups also
offering to provide practical services, psychologists could
claim that their methods for achieving adjustment of the client
to the environment were based on *science* (Napoli 1981).

This academic emphasis had two important results influencing the status of women in psychology: it excluded women
from positions of power even in those areas where they were
most numerous, and it conferred upon applied psychology
lower status. Control of the field of psychology, including its
applied subfields, continued to be held by persons with academic positions, especially at the prestigious universities. And,
despite the fact that the first three decades of the twentieth
century were generally the "heyday" for academic women

(Bernard 1964), it was openly acknowledged that in psychology relatively few academic positions were as yet open to women. Actually, a full 40 percent of the women members of APA in 1928 reported giving no instruction; for men the figure was 14 percent (Fernberger 1928). Ten years later women still had restricted access to academic posts: "If one is a man, he has 75 chances out of 100 of getting an academic job after psychological training. But if one is a woman, her chances of obtaining an academic position of any rank whatsoever are reduced to less than 40 chances out of 100" (Fernberger 1939:390). Thus the "persons with academic positions" referred to above were in fact men, and women were unable to enter employment situations that were associated with power and influence in the field.

A second consequence of the continued dominance of psychology by academics was that applied work came to be regarded as a second-class activity. Attitudes of the day are expressed in an account written in 1913: "Clinical psychology has so far proved of interest to only a very small percentage of the students and teachers of psychology and what is still more to the point, very few of those who are interested in clinical psychology take it seriously" (H. H. Goddard 1913, cited in Napoli 1981:56). Though more people began to take it seriously, its status among psychologists remained low. One individual who sought to remedy this condition complained that positions in the clinical field were viewed as "second-string jobs" (J. E. Wallace Wallin 1930, cited in Napoli 1981:57). A university-based man observed at a meeting of clinical psychologists in 1933 that applied psychology was "not the work for a man" (Napoli 1981:56). Applied psychology was something that academic men did a bit of research on or engaged in as a sideline, but it became the *primary* work of most employed women psychologists.

The devaluation of applied psychology may have resulted in part from the very fact that women were there in the majority. Work done by women, then as now, was considered less important, less worthy than work done by men.[2] Commenting on this situation, a historian of applied psychology noted:

A curious situation arose that did not augur well for the professional-ization of applied psychology. Men comprised over two-thirds of all American psychologists in 1930, but they made up a distinct minor-ity of applied psychologists. . . . Even without consciously discrimi-nating against them men may have categorized applied psychologists as sub-professionals like social workers and elementary school teachers simply because most practitioners were women. (Napoli 1981:47)

Another possible reason for the lower status of applied psy-chology during the 1920s and 1930s was that the activities involved were associated with traditional feminine concerns: child and family welfare, education, nurturance, and guidance. Further, the work was viewed as menial. Applied psycholo-gists, even those with Ph.D.s, usually worked in staff posi-tions, under managerial supervision rather than as autonomous professionals, situations consistent with the subordinate role assigned to women. Further, work in these fields often in-volved direct contact with needy people, and as historians Brumberg and Tomes point out in a review essay on women and professionalization, those in "high status professions do not maintain close contact with their clients; philosophical ab-straction and distance from human complications characterize their elite cadres" (1982:288).[3]

With training in all areas eventually open to women, why did so many choose the applied specialities—thereby establish-ing these as women's work? A good case might be made for the appeal of applied psychology to women's genuine inter-ests. It offered them the opportunity to pursue the idealistic goal of service and to become deeply and meaningfully en-gaged in contributing to the welfare of other people. Also, from the 1920s on, applied psychology provided the most accessible way for women to enter and remain within the boundaries of psychology, as it involved work that was con-gruent with women's social role.

And finally the observation of a woman psychologist in 1938 that "as a teaching profession, psychology was, and still is largely a man's field" (Gertrude Hildreth cited in Frith

1939:1) remained an accurate characterization for many decades hence. So those women who truly preferred academic psychology and had a "vocation for teaching," when forced to make a realistic appraisal of their prospects, might well have adjusted their goals and turned instead to applied work, to become practitioners rather than professors and researchers. It is not possible to determine for earlier periods whether women entered applied psychology in such impressive numbers because this was what they really wanted or because it was the work they could get and were willing to take. Quite possibly in many cases both of these explanations applied.

An influential psychologist—who had some years earlier been secretary of the APA—voiced a prevalent attitude in his ingenuous introduction to an article referred to earlier in this chapter:

The following analysis was initiated by the decision of a woman graduate student to seek an academic career in psychology, inasmuch as she was not interested in a position in the applied fields. The author held out small hopes for success and told her that he suspected that there were much better opportunities for a woman in a career in applied psychology. The student, in order to answer this argument, discovered that more than 250 women [compared with more than 1200 men], who were Members or Associates of the [APA], were in academic positions of one sort or another. This number was so much larger than the author had expected that a more detailed analysis of the situation seemed advisable. (Fernberger 1939:390)

Whether because of personal goals, a perception of more hospitable acceptance, or direct advice, women doctoral students became concentrated in those programs that produced applied specialists (Finison and Furumoto 1980). It comes as no surprise then that a 1939 paper on growth trends in the profession stated that "among the persons who have recently entered the consulting and applied fields, the women outnumber the men" (Gertrude Hildreth cited in Frith 1939:1).

The growth of applied psychology thus presented women both an advantage and a handicap. While it offered employment opportunities for individuals who would otherwise have been shut out of the field, it also created a distinctive type of work in which women were the majority of employees. The identification of applied psychology as "women's work" was problematical, for men as well as women, because, as such, it was less highly regarded than "men's work"—scientific and theoretical psychology housed in academia.

Women, however, tended not only to accept this situation but also to express satisfaction with it. A comprehensive survey of about five hundred women Ph.D.s matched with a sample of men was conducted in 1946, when women constituted about one-third of all psychologists (Bryan and Boring 1947). At that time women held 60 percent of psychological positions in practical professional work—in schools, educational systems, clinics, guidance centers, hospitals, and custodial institutions. The women surveyed reported that they preferred the kinds of jobs they actually had, while they acknowledged that on average women were paid less for their work than men. Both women and men liked their profession and expressed no regrets for what they had done in it. The women were almost as satisfied as the men, despite the fact that both men and women agreed that there was much more prejudice against women and that women were at a disadvantage professionally, though they recognized that in certain areas it was helpful to be woman. Men not only were paid more; they got work more easily, lacked the marriage-profession conflict, and achieved more. Men and women expressed equal satisfaction with marriage, but whereas three-fourths of the men reported that marriage helped their career advancement, only one-third of the women did so.

LATER WOMEN PSYCHOLOGISTS

In addition to the rise of applied psychology, a second major change that may have been observed by the first generation of woman psychologists as they approached the end of their careers was the appearance of a new type of woman in the field. Younger women did not experience the same educational barriers, were likely to hold a different attitude toward the marriage-career dilemma, and though hesitant to identify themselves as feminists, were more alert to the need to band with other women to combat male dominance.

Women who were born into middle-class families around the turn of the century came to view higher education for themselves as a given, to be pursued as a matter of course. The generation preceding them had successfully broken the barriers to advanced education and training. Basking in the belief that the battles for equality had been won, later women generally lacked the defiant spirit that had energized late nineteenth-century women. An educated woman was no longer a rarity, and she was no longer considered unsuited for marriage. Indeed, during the 1920s a college education came to be regarded as a prerequisite for homemaking. Housewifery itself took on the status of a career and motherhood became a "profession."[4]

Among trained psychologists, however, more women of the new generation chose to pursue professional careers *in addition to* marriage and homemaking. Whereas earlier women had generally submitted to the marriage-or-career dictum, significant numbers of women now believed that the choice was not an either-or proposition and determined to combine the two, to enlarge "women's sphere" by incorporating the career. As the older women had lacked models for engaging in professional work, so these younger women lacked examples for the combined roles they undertook. Thus they too became pioneers. The women who successfully accomplished the balancing act did so by using a wide variety of coping strategies and served as models for those following them. Flexible and persistent, they made accommodations in both the wife-mother and career aspects of their lives, taking advantage of opportunities to use whatever resources were available.[5]

These "second-generation" women psychologists had considerable confidence in their abilities to achieve in the profession. Their motto may have been "dig in and prove yourself." One of them recalled that her generation believed it was their main duty, as women professionals, to show that women could, in fact, do what the early pioneers claimed they could do: "that women could serve effectively as doctors and lawyers and as scholars and college and university professors and also in responsible positions in business and government" (Edna Heidbreder, interview by Furumoto, 1977). Another said: "We just wanted to be good psychologists" (Lucy Day Boring, interview by Scarborough, 1976). Yet another: "You don't want to do things as a woman, but as a person" (Edith Mulhall Achilles, interview by Scarborough, 1979).

These women were clearly acting on strong personal motivations. We do not know, however, whether they felt that simply doing the work was sufficient reward, or whether they also desired professional recognition and had enough faith in the notion of meritocracy to believe that this would eventually come to them. Whatever injustices they encountered they seem to have minimized and perceived usually as barriers to be overcome individually, as did Margaret Washburn (see chapter 4). Not sensitized to think systematically in terms of discrimination, they tended not to see it in their own lives, and this blindness may have been a temporarily effective coping strategy.

Yet it was this later generation that mounted the first group effort to confront issues of equality and discrimination. The impetus came from the blatant exclusion of women from activities for which they felt themselves especially qualified. In 1939 the APA set up the Emergency Committee in Psychology in response to a growing concern about the war in Europe. Recalling their successes during World War I, psychologists were preparing to contribute to the burgeoning national defense effort. Women believed that they had unusual expertise in certain war-related issues, particularly those of the home front. No women, however, were appointed to the Emergency Committee. At the APA convention the next year (1940), women psychologists met separately to generate an organized program for their participation in the war plans. They were blocked in their efforts to be included in APA's activities—and some became mobilized by their outrage. In December 1941, recognizing that "strength lay in union," a small group of women met and decided to organize on a national scale. Within six months the National Council of Women Psychologists (NCWP) became an active organization to promote the contributions of women in psychology, especially as they related to the war effort. Even those women who were most deeply involved in the NCWP activities, however, were often ambivalent about how they should deal with feminist issues, notably the Equal Rights Amendment, which the group refused to support. Most insisted on limiting their focus to strictly professional concerns.[6]

FERMENT OF THE 1970S

Not until the 1970s did women's concerns gain attention in the affairs of professional psychology. With the nationwide rise of a new tide of feminism, women psychologists, along with women in other professions, moved to institute specific measures for improving their status. First, and most dramatic, was the formation in 1969 of the Association for Women in Psychology (AWP) as an activist group operating outside the APA. This was followed by the APA's establishing a Task Force on the Status of Women in 1970 and then a continuing Committee on Women in Psychology (CWP) in 1973. The CWP was charged to further the purpose of the APA—advancing psychology as a science and a means of promoting human welfare—by "ensuring that women achieve equality as members of the psychological community, in order that all human resources be fully actualized" (Committee on Women in Psychology 1984:1).[7] In 1977 the Women's Program Office was established as a part of the APA's central organization. Further strengthening the position of women was the formation in 1973 of the Division of Psychology of Women (Division 35) in the APA to represent the interests of that particular subfield. Thus the last fifteen years have seen highly visible structural changes, which acknowledge the presence of women in psychology and enhance their professional identity. This period has not been without difficulties and setbacks, however. The decision to hold annual APA meetings only in states that had ratified the Equal Rights Amendment fueled a backlash directed not only against the amendment but also against other efforts to improve the status of women in the field. In 1981 the APA membership rejected by a near two-to-one vote a by-law amendment to establish a standing Board of Women's Issues.[8]

What is the present status of women psychologists? In 1981 women in the APA reported major fields spanning the breadth of the discipline. They were most heavily represented in the developmental (50.3 percent women), school (47.2 percent), clinical (30.0 percent), educational (29.2 percent), and consulting (28.0 percent) areas of psychology. Over the period from 1920 to 1974, women received 22.7 percent of all U.S. doctoral degrees in psychology. The proportions of doctorates going to women began to climb in the 1970s, and in 1983 women earned 47.5 percent of the doctoral degrees granted in psychology—taking more than half of the doctorates in the subfields of psychometrics, developmental psychology and gerontology, school psychology, and social psychology. In 1984 women constituted 32.8 percent of the APA membership. Women's recognition and participation in the activities of the APA have increased dramatically, so that in 1984 they were approaching representation on boards, committees, and task forces equivalent to their proportion of the membership, having even exceeded this in some areas (Committee on Women in Psychology, 1984).

WOMEN IN HISTORY OF PSYCHOLOGY

As we have shown, women have been an important part of psychology's past. They have not, however, been included in psychology's history. As documented in the introduction, neither the women nor their work is acknowledged in current historical writing. Earlier we spoke of how history in general has ignored women. Here we focus on issues specific to the history of psychology.

A number of explanations may account for the absence of women in the history of psychology. Historians have focused mainly on *intellectual history,* viewing psychology as a science rather than a profession and tracing the development of ideas and theory, which are of primary concern to academic psychology. This approach neglects the academic vs. applied issue that has plagued twentieth-century psychology. Ignoring the social history of the field and its applied aspects eliminates most women psychologists, for women were more prominent in the applied areas. Psychology's historians have also tended to take a *presentist approach,* judging certain earlier work, although important in its time, as not relevant to today's concerns and therefore not worthy of consideration in historical accounts.[9] Because much of the work of the early women was done in a mode that has been superseded by later theory and methods, they and their contributions are eliminated.

Texts also show evidence of a *filtering function,* in which later writers rely heavily on earlier ones, gradually dropping certain subjects and persons from discussion while coming to a consensus on what history of psychology should include. This tendency has contributed to the loss of women psychologists as successive accounts have made less and less mention of them; works written during the lifetimes of the women tend to portray more accurately the breadth and importance of their contributions. Still another explanation may be found in the *obliteration phenomenon* identified by Garfield (1975) to describe the failure of scientists to give credit to the originator of an idea or technique that has become widely accepted.[10] And finally, we cannot overlook *prejudice against women and women's work*—a topic discussed earlier in this chapter. Devaluation of whatever is produced by women continues as a widespread though often unacknowledged attitude. There is little reason to believe that historians are exempted from this cultural handicap.

These may be explanations. They are not, however, justifications for the exclusion of women psychologists from historical accounts. A history of psychology that ignores women is at best only a partial truth—both distorted and incomplete. To achieve a fuller portrayal of psychology's past, we must look carefully at all of its founders and practitioners, those who contributed to its birth and those who nurtured its development. We will take a step in that direction when the untold lives of women psychologists—their presence, contributions, and experience—become an integral part of the history of their discipline.

Cameo Portraits of Selected Women

Kate Gordon Moore (1878–1963)

The daughter of a physician in Oshkosh, Wisconsin, Kate Gordon studied at the Wisconsin State Normal School there and then entered the University of Chicago, where she received her bachelor's degree in 1900 and her doctorate in 1903. The following year Gordon studied in Germany at Würzburg on an ACA fellowship. Returning to the United States in 1904, she served on the faculties of Mt. Holyoke College (1904–1906), Teachers College, Columbia (1906–1907), Bryn Mawr College (1912–1916), and Carnegie Institute of Technology (1916–1921) before settling in Los Angeles at the University of California. (Presumably she returned to her family during the five-year break between 1907 and 1912, as records give an Oshkosh address for her in 1910.) During these early years she taught a wide range of courses in psychology, philosophy, and education and did research on memory, attention, vision, aesthetics, and mental testing of children. She also published textbooks on aesthetics and educational psychology.

Gordon joined the faculty at UCLA as an associate professor shortly after it changed from a teacher's college to the southern branch of the University of California. Her first years there were a period of especially prolific scholarship and publishing for Gordon. Nevertheless, it is likely she would have remained at the associate professor level (as did her colleague, psychologist Grace Fernald) except for an untimely death in 1933 that left the department without a chairperson just as it was authorized to initiate graduate work. As there were no senior-ranking men in the department, Gordon was appointed chair until the suitable man could be found in 1935. During her year as chair, she was promoted to professor at the age of fifty-six.

Gordon was one of the few first-generation women psychologists who had the experience of instructing male students. One of them, a psychologist in private practice at the time of her death, wrote of meeting her in 1942 and of his deep admiration:

I was enormously impressed with her charm and erudition (we talked about art, and then conversed in Spanish a little) and she immediately carried for me an image of a fine, scholarly lady—just the sort of person I had hoped I would find at the University as a professor. . . . [Later] I took two of her classes and was delighted with them. . . . I remember with gratitude, and also with nostalgia, the fine lady who was both scientist and scholar, and never lost sight of the fact that the psyche was something to be appreciated, even loved, and not just an object for study and use. (Fisher et al. 1965)

In 1943, five years before her retirement, Kate Gordon married Ernest Carroll Moore, the man who might be considered the founder of UCLA. The marriage lasted until his death in 1955 and from all indications greatly enriched their later lives. Moore had received the Ph.D. from Chicago five years earlier than Gordon; they had both been students of John Dewey. After teaching at Berkeley, Harvard, and Yale, he had become president of the Los Angeles State Normal School in 1917 and presided as chief administrator when that institute was elevated to the status of a university. Moore's first wife, Dorothea Rhodes Lummis, was a physician more than ten years older than he and died in 1942 after years of invalidism. In his journal Moore chronicled the years when Gordon was a close friend of the couple in Los Angeles and regularly visited them for dinner and to take him for drives in her car along the coast. After his wife's death, Moore gave Gordon his wife's ring, "as Dorothea had wished her to have it" (Ernest Carroll Moore Journal, March 13, 1942, ECMP). A year later they were married and he declared, "I have begun to live again and it is this good woman who has done it all" (March 7, 1943). He also recorded that she, a bride at age sixty-five, was visibly moved and shaking when she "said her lines" during the wedding ceremony, and he speculated that she was probably nervous about returning to the classroom. Three weeks later he wrote, "I rejoice every time now that Kate Gordon Moore can not drop me at my door and drive off but that she puts up her car and stays!" (March 27, 1943).

Lillien Jane Martin (1851–1943)

Lillien Martin did not take up doctoral study in psychology until midlife. Prior to this she was a public school teacher; subsequently she became a professor of psychology and finally after retiring from academic life, a consulting psychologist. Born into a prominent family that had helped establish a small town in the southwestern corner of New York state, she entered the Olean Academy at age four. Her father, educated at Geneva College, never settled into his father's business and eventually abandoned his family. Her mother, reportedly an enterprising woman, then became the family's source of support and moved with her children to Wisconsin where, as matron in a private preparatory school for boys, she was able to provide for the education of her sons. Lillien, the oldest child and only daughter, went to teach at a nearby girls' school but soon left for a teaching post in Nebraska. It was not until 1876, when she was twenty-five, that she had earned enough to support her college study, a long-time goal. She aspired to enter Cornell, which was near her birthplace, but her mother objected to that plan when the university replied to her application by saying: "We have not yet received an application for a female, but we see no reason to oppose it" (deFord 1948:22). Mrs. Martin did not want her daughter to be the only young woman at Cornell. Lillien then journeyed from Nebraska to Poughkeepsie, New York, where she took entrance examinations at Vassar College and was surprised to win a four-year scholarship. After graduating in 1880, she accepted a post in a high school in Indianapolis, where she taught physics and chemistry. Nine years later she moved to San Francisco, where she was vice-principal and head of the science department of the Girls' High School.

During the early 1890s, Martin came across the work of Wilhelm Wundt and became interested in the field of psychology. Then in 1894, while on summer vacation, she became fascinated with the writings of Thèodule Armand Ribot, a French psychologist whose views were similar to her own. When she remarked to her companion that she wanted to "really study" psychology, the friend encouraged her: "Well, if you want to, why don't you?" (deFord 1948:38). Martin acted immediately. She consulted with professors at the University of California, determined to go to Germany to study, and resigned her position. While the sudden decision to make such a momentous life change at age forty-four seems implausible, the death of her mother some time before had released her from the family claim and freed her to make a major move. Earlier she had been supporting her mother and spending her long teacher's vacations in Indianapolis because her mother refused to live in San Francisco.

Martin arrived in Göttingen before the 1894 fall term began and remained in Germany for four years, though Göttingen was not awarding Ph.D.s to women at that time. Her ties to the German psychology centers continued, and she returned on several occasions—to Würzburg, to Bonn, and to Munich—and was awarded an honorary Ph.D. from the University of Bonn in 1913, a singular distinction.

In 1898 Martin joined the faculty at Stanford University, where the president was David Starr Jordan, a long-time friend who had helped her gain the Indianapolis appointment. She rose through the academic ranks and in 1915 became the first woman to head a Stanford department, all the while conducting and publishing her research. In 1916, at age sixty-five, she was required to retire. An extremely energetic woman, she then began another career, an entirely new venture that lasted ten years longer than her academic tenure. During these years, in addition to conducting a private practice, she worked first with children in mental hygiene clinics and then in gerontology—a field she helped establish.

One of Martin's biographers commented: "She lived self-improvement." The activity theory that she espoused as a way of avoiding the negative effects of aging was demonstrated by her own life:

She gained national publicity by traveling alone to Russia at seventy-eight, making a coast-to-coast automobile tour at eighty-one, and then at eighty-seven taking a six months' tour of South America. In her eighth decade she learned to drive, and when her handwriting was no longer steady she taught herself touch typing. (Burnham 1971a:504)

A partial explanation for Martin's prodigious accomplishments is given in a brief epitaph: "She died as young as she was born. Age ninety-one. And all through those years, she was born every morning" (Walter Pitkin, cited in deFord 1948:119).

Naomi Norsworthy (1877–1916)

Naomi Norsworthy's dependence on her mother and Mrs. Norsworthy's possessiveness and reliance on her daughter as a young confidant may be explained in several ways. Naomi was born in New York City just two years after her mother moved from England in 1875 to marry an engineer who had migrated earlier to America. The couple had lost their first child, and the grieving, homesick young mother, who never lost her allegiance to her homeland, poured all the vitality of her forceful character into caring for Naomi and the two sons who soon followed. Further, Naomi seemed to be the fulfillment of a wish made by her paternal grandmother, whom her mother had cared for prior to marriage: that the mother might have a daughter who could provide the strength and comfort for her that she herself had given to her future mother-in-law. The elder Mrs. Norsworthy had made a great impression on Naomi's mother, who converted to the older woman's evangelical religion and in turn imparted her religious fervor to her daughter Naomi. The tenets of the Plymouth Brethren, which emphasized selfless duty and service, and devotion to her mother became dominant features of Naomi's life.

The daughter was well trained in domestic skills as a girl, but her play time was spent with her younger brothers, whose activities she greatly enjoyed—to the extent that her father nicknamed her "Boy." Mrs. Norsworthy determined to provide educational advantages for all her children and carefully supervised their studies and religious upbringing. Naomi entered the public school in Rutherford, New Jersey, at age eight and completed her studies there in seven years. Her strong desire to be a teacher led her to enter the New Jersey State Normal School at Trenton. At fifteen she was younger than the other students and poorly prepared in several subjects because she had had no high school training. Nevertheless, she completed her course in three years and for the next three years taught the third grade in Morristown, New Jersey.

Norsworthy nurtured an ambition to earn a college degree from Columbia University's Teachers College in New York City. When she was able to enroll there in 1899, her mother moved the family back to the city. The following year she was appointed student assistant in psychology, beginning sixteen years of service to Teachers College. She received her B.S. in 1901 and her Ph.D. in 1904. As a member of the Teachers College faculty, Norsworthy taught a majority of the courses given in psychology, both graduate and undergraduate. She was a gifted, inspiring teacher. Her classes were large; she spoke once of meeting 480 different students in a given week. In addition to her faculty duties, she was adviser of women and deeply involved in fostering the student social and religious organizations at Teachers College and Columbia University. She received offers from other institutions but felt very certain her ordained place was at Teachers College, where she believed she could have closer contact with students. To a friend she wrote, "I must have the inner consciousness of doing things that satisfy, and that I believe I will more nearly have here at Teachers College" (Higgins 1918:202).

Norsworthy did not find teaching always an easy or even pleasant task. She often had to substitute for her department head in his absence. When this happened unexpectedly quite early in her career, she overheard a student in the front row remark to his neighbor at the beginning of the class period: "Where is the professor today? and who is this in his place? I, for one, did not come to Teachers College to be taught by a chit of a girl." Her usual shyness and self-deprecation vanished in response to the comment, and at the close of the hour the objector told her that he had enjoyed the session. "I never felt more giddy with victory in my life," she later commented (Higgins 1918:78–79). Teaching men was an unnerving experience for Norsworthy as seen in an undated letter in which she wrote:

I wish I could creep into some little backwoods village and be lost so I wouldn't have to teach graduate classes with men in them that don't want to be taught by a woman. . . . I wish I could be a rural school teacher in the deepest of the Wilds for just a bit of a time! (Higgins 1918:191)

But Norsworthy's "foolish natural shrinking," as she referred to it, and the intimidating sexism of male students did not prevent her from being an extraordinarily effective teacher and faculty advisor. On one occasion a student who had been strongly advised by others to register for her courses felt he had been cheated when he discovered the professor was "a slip of a woman." When he appealed to the dean,

His complaint was listened to patiently and fully,—that he had been misled into registering for a course with Dr. Norsworthy under the assumption that the Doctor was a man, and she was not at all. The dean finally told him that he was still laboring under some sort of false impression,—"You will find her one of the strongest men on our faculty. Go to her classes a few times and see if you do not think her so." This story is rounded out by the man's returning to the dean in the course of time to assure him that his opinion concerning Dr. Norsworthy as one of the "strong men" of the faculty was entirely true. (Higgins 1918:80)

Throughout these years Norsworthy, though never in good health, combined the role of "daughter at home" with graduate study and professional work. She took charge of her family's household management to relieve her mother of the burden. This included rising early to serve her mother breakfast in bed and tidying the apartment before leaving the house each morning and returning from a full day's work to prepare the evening meal. During her mother's two-year struggle with terminal cancer, Norsworthy personally attended to her, simultaneously dispatching her many duties at Teachers College though she herself was seriously ill with cancer by the time her mother died. She managed to teach for another year, then was forced to take a semester's leave and died in December 1916. Her most enduring publication was *The Psychology of Childhood* (Norsworthy and Whitley 1918), which was designed as a normal school text and completed after her death by a devoted colleague.

Frances Hall Rousmaniere Dewing (1876–1964)

Frances Rousmaniere was the daughter of a prosperous businessman in the Boston area. Her college years were interrupted by the illness of her younger brother. Because her mother suffered from heart trouble, Rousmaniere left school to help nurse him. In 1900 she received her B.A. from Wellesley, where she developed a lifelong friendship with Mary Calkins. More than sixty years later, she wrote: "The effort at the college seemed to be to turn our interests outward, toward general improvement of the country and the world, or outward to other chances for going on further in academic work" (Notes for letter to Mrs. Mansfield, n.d., FRDP). When her mother died in 1903, shortly after her father's death, Rousmaniere went to live with the family of a Harvard medical school professor in Cambridge and began graduate study at Radcliffe College, where she earned a Ph.D. in 1906. Her graduate study in philosophy was motivated by the personal pleasure of learning rather than any professional goal; she enjoyed the work and applied for the degree only at the urging of George Herbert Palmer and Josiah Royce, Harvard professors who saw that she had acquired enough courses to qualify. Nevertheless, she taught for four years, first at Mt. Holyoke and then at Smith, before marrying Arthur Dewing, a professor at Simmons College and Harvard University business school whom she had met at Harvard. They settled in Cambridge where the births of three daughters followed in quick succession during the next six years.

Like many faculty wives, Rousmaniere helped her husband with business matters and writing professional articles. She disliked women's clubs, considering them too impersonal, and found that their activities were not intellectually satisfying for her. Her life came to revolve around her family and a few close friends. She turned her intellectual energy to such pursuits as encouraging the children's learning through use of Montessori objects and devising more efficient and satisfying means of housekeeping in the absence of a "general housework girl." She took her family responsibilities very seriously and domesticity became a major theme, though she did keep up relationships with her former instructors and had close rapport with intellectuals in the community through her husband's faculty connections.

Rousmaniere recorded many of her ideas as she puzzled about how to accomplish her goals for living. Her musings indicate the domestic problems confronting a middle-class wife in the early twentieth century and her struggle to resolve them while acknowledging the needs of all family members. During the first years of her marriage, she made notes about these problems (FRDP). Concerning the lack of suitable household help, she wrote:

Simplify your way of living, let everyone in the family do a little of the work, and have good service come in by the hour or day, as your needs require. . . . I propose this winter to get breakfast for my family myself, and to have each member serve himself from the kitchen stove, whenever he chooses to have breakfast. For that meal, we shall eat in the kitchen so that the table may be left til the "clearer up" comes, without giving an effect of untidiness to the house. . . . Each member of the household is to be responsible for the daily care of his or her room—except the babies. . . . And when I am washing dishes, I hope it will be possible for my husband to read aloud to me—often, if not always.

She noted regarding husband-wife relations:

After marriage, wife's business is bearing and rearing children—housekeeping comes as it may to fit conditions . . . wife must keep her vitality and life and interest in things for sake of the present—and general justice of personal relations, efficiency as mother. Good to keep alive and develop a fad or profession to put life into again when children are grown and away. . . . Husband helps as he can. . . . Rightly, husbands "career" is one of four coordinate claims—other than wife's life, children's life, his own. . . . Ambition for social position often pushes a wife to push her husband to sacrifice too much for his career. Support is due from him, and more—cooperation, but not for social position necessarily.

On education for women she noted:

Seldom is it necessary or really valuable to the home that the mother has standing in any profession, or has achieved distinction in any field. In so far as that has enriched the mother's life and character it is a vital contribution to a home, but generally speaking homes are real homes for children rather in spite of their mother's success outside than because of it . . . . For [girls], even more than for boys, it is dangerous to stretch the period of preparation, because . . . their own lives are complicated by the consciousness of the uncertainty of their future and another hunger less deliberately planned for, the hunger for personal service, of some living thing dependent upon them.

Rousmaniere believed that girls are hungry for "the chance to bring something real to pass which shall indicate their value in the world" and that motherhood and homemaking should fill that hunger. And yet domestic activities, despite the energy she poured into them, did not fully satisfy her. She wrote her notes out of another need, the need to keep mentally alert: "I decided last night that I must keep a journal—and think out something worth writing in it every day—drifting into acceptance of doing a lot of housework—but I feel hungry all the time, and this seems the way to get partly around it" (Journal, May 24, 1913, FRDP). But: "When Arthur is home there is no time for journal writing. We talk instead" (Journal, May 28, 1913, FRDP).

Rousmaniere's continuing efforts to sort things out are chronicled in notes to her former Wellesley classmates in the class books that were published at five-year intervals (Records of the Class of 1898, WCA). In 1913 she wrote:

I have lived in Cambridge, struggled with housekeeping, become acquainted with 2 mites of young ladies and done a very little teaching as assistant in a course in psychology and ethics which Mr. Dewing gives at Simmons. I am in excellent health and spirits, though at times bewildered by the multiplicity of claims of "modern" life. (Classbook of 1913:60, WCA)

Twenty years later she declared: "I do nothing notable along civic and other lines, much less than my interests would lead to. Ordinary living challenges all my resources so far, especially in this puzzling world of today" (Classbook of 1933:55, WCA).

Despite the fact that she was often perplexed about the changes required by modern life, Rousmaniere returned to teaching during World War II, at age sixty-seven. In 1942 she took a position at Bennington College in Vermont, where one of her daughters had been a student during the 1930s. Her husband was supportive of this decision, though he remained in Cambridge. Her younger sister's illness made her decide to terminate the appointment, but for three years Rousmaniere helped cover the home front by teaching college mathematics, as she had at Mt. Holyoke almost forty years earlier.

Theodate Louise Smith (1859–1914)

Theodate Smith was born in 1859 in Hallowell, Maine, and received bachelor's and master's degrees from Smith College (1882 and 1884). After leaving Smith she was employed for several years teaching in female seminaries, private secondary schools for "young ladies." Then in 1893 she entered Yale University where she earned a Ph.D. in 1896. Her mentor was E.W. Scripture, a Leipzig Ph.D. who had strong interests in both experimental psychology and education, particularly the scientific study of the child's mind. Smith's doctoral research examined the relationship between motor activity and memory and demonstrated that psychology had practical applications in pedagogy. Completing her research in 1895, she spent a year at Clark University attending lectures on topics in education. She then returned to teach for two years at the Mt. Vernon Seminary in Washington, D.C., while also attending classes at Catholic University. In 1899 she continued her postdoctoral education at Cornell.

In 1902 Smith became a research assistant to G. Stanley Hall at Clark University, the center of the burgeoning child study movement that Hall was vigorously promoting. While Hall was president at Clark he was also engaged in extensive research projects, and Smith became his coauthor on many of the reports that emerged from these studies. Hall was a difficult man, ambitious and self-centered (Ross 1972). Though capable of inspiring strong loyalty in his subordinates, he nevertheless treated them, both men and women, in a supercilious manner. He also maintained and espoused a rigidly traditional view of woman's role.

Smith appears to have shared Hall's views, articulated in a jointly authored paper on marriage and parenting (Hall and Smith 1903). Her attitude was consonant with the ethos that operated at Smith College during her undergraduate days and emphasized women's talents and abilities as being quite different from men's (see Gordon 1975). Apparently her pursuit of advanced education was motivated not by ambitions to achieve professional status but rather by intellectual interests combined with a desire to be of service to humanity in ways uniquely fitted to the feminine character. It was perhaps their likeness of mind on the issue of woman's proper place that allowed Hall to tolerate Smith as an anomaly among educated women and write in her obituary:

Few have ever better illustrated the law of service. . . . Although a woman of such ability must have smarted to see her juniors and inferiors advance above her in position and salary, this bitter experience, so common in cultivated women, never modified her opinion concerning woman's place and function in modern society, and her views on these questions . . . testified both to her conservatism and to the judicial quality of her mind. (Hall 1914:160)

In 1909 Smith became lecturer and librarian at the newly established Children's Institute at Clark, a position she held until her sudden death in 1914. During her last years, her interests turned to child welfare issues. She traveled in Europe investigating children's institutions and became a widely recognized interpreter for the American audience of Maria Montessori's educational practices.

Helen Bradford Thompson Woolley (1874–1947)

Supported by a coterie of sympathetic men at the University of Chicago, Helen Thompson conducted one of the first comprehensive experimental studies of sex differences. For her doctoral research, she tackled the issue of sex differences in mental abilities. Repeatedly she found similarities rather than differences in the males and females she examined. Where differences were identified, she showed how experience and rearing rather than biology might account for them (Thompson 1903). Rosalind Rosenberg (1982: ch. 3) provides an excellent discussion of Thompson and her work and notes that after her marriage she "lived almost exclusively in a world of women whose concerns and goals became her concerns and goals" (83). Thompson's biographers record her contributions to bettering "the lives of women and children through improvements in family life, education, welfare, and social legislation" (Zapoleon and Stolz 1971:660).

Helen Thompson was born in Chicago. Her parents strongly supported education for women, and their three daughters all attended college. She was a brilliant student at the University of Chicago, receiving her undergraduate degree in 1897 and her Ph.D. in 1900. After a year in Europe on a fellowship granted by the Association of Collegiate Alumnae, she returned to take a faculty position at Mt. Holyoke College, where she directed the psychological laboratory. At the time she was a graduate student, she had become engaged to Paul G. Woolley. Though he had reservations, which accounted for their long engagement, his parents pushed for the marriage. The couple were wedded in 1905 in Japan. He was then director of a laboratory in the Philippine Islands. During the next several years, the couple moved four times and finally settled in Cincinnati when he was appointed to the University of Cincinnati medical school faculty.

Thompson taught as instructor in philosophy from 1910 to 1912 at Cincinnati, but in 1911 she began a project that set a new direction for her work. She became director of the Bureau for the Investigation of Working Children, which evolved into the Cincinnati Vocation Bureau. Under Thompson's guidance the bureau produced significant research reports on the effects of child labor, and Thompson became a powerful proponent of child welfare reform and an influential community leader. In 1921 the Woolley family, which by then included two daughters (born in 1907 and 1914), moved to Detroit where Paul was associated with the Detroit College of Medicine. Helen was then appointed to the staff of the Merrill-Palmer School. There she organized one of the first nursery schools in the country for the study of child development and the training of teachers and conducted research on the mental abilities of young children.

The couple had always lived separate lives, spending their summers apart, and in 1924 Paul Woolley left for a tuberculosis sanitarium in California. The following year, when she was fifty, Thompson accepted a significant career opportunity and moved to become director of the new Institute of Child Welfare Research and professor of education at Teachers College, Columbia University. During her first year in New York she was highly successful in getting the institute established, but multiple personal traumas took their toll. An account of the difficulties she experienced during this period of her life was contained in a letter written by her daughter Eleanor to Rosalind Rosenberg in 1976. She had been sustained, both in Cincinnati and in Detroit, by intimate women friends. In New York she was separated from them and her daughters, who were away at school. Just before the move, she underwent a hysterectomy and at the same time had to deal with a friend's terminal cancer and the realization that the separation from her husband would be permanent. In 1926 Thompson became emotionally incapacitated, and she was required to take a leave from her new position. When she returned two years later, it was still impossible for her to work effectively. Forced to resign in 1930, she moved into Eleanor's household where she spent the remaining seventeen years of her life.

Published Sources of Biographical Information

Biographical information on the first-generation women psychologists may be found in several standard sources, identified in the list by the following code. The women's names are given as they appear in table 6.1. Where a biographical entry appears under another name for a woman who married, that name is indicated in parentheses. A summary of biographical data on most of the women is provided in Furumoto and Scarborough (1986).

DAB	*Dictionary of American Biography*
NAW	*Notable American Women*
NCAB	*National Cyclopedia of American Biography*
PR	*Psychological Register (vol. 3, 1932)*
WWWA	*Woman's Who's Who of America (1914–1915)*

Name	*Biographical Source*
Adams	WWWA
Allen	PR (Charters)
Bagley	WWWA
Calkins	DAB, NAW, NCAB, PR, WWWA
Case	—
Franklin	DAB, NAW, NCAB, PR (all Ladd-Franklin)
Gamble	PR, WWWA
Gordon	PR
Hamlin	NCAB, WWWA (both Hinman)
McKeag	WWWA
Martin	NAW, NCAB, PR, WWWA

Moore	—
Norsworthy	DAB, WWWA
Prichard	—
Puffer	WWWA (Howes)
Rousmaniere	—
Rowland	PR (Wembridge)
Shinn	NAW, WWWA
Smith, M. K.	PR, WWWA
Smith, T. L.	DAB, WWWA
Squire	WWWA
Talbot	NCAB, PR, WWWA
Thompson	NAW, PR, WWWA (all Woolley)
Washburn	DAB, NAW, NCAB, PR, WWWA
Williams	PR (Kemmerer)

Notes

Introduction

1. A colleague at Wellesley College, Claire Zimmerman, has called to our attention a recent telling example of how women psychologists and their contributions to the discipline can be obliterated. In this instance an introductory psychology textbook describing studies on concept formation carried out by Edna Heidbreder in the 1940s misidentifies the researcher as "Alfred Heidbreder" (Darley, Glucksberg, and Kinchla 1981:274).

2. See Bledstein (1976) for a discussion of the values associated with the professional role that developed in the late 1800s. The goal of "autonomous individualism," a central feature of this role, conflicted sharply with women's traditional roles of submissiveness and dependency. This posed a problem for women who aspired to be professionals similar to the problem faced by women scientists.

3. See Camfield (1973) for a more detailed account of the professionalization of American psychology that took place between 1870 and 1917.

4. Cattell (1917) said that he had counted up the number of women in his directory *American Men of Science* (presumably the second edition, which appeared in 1910) and found the following percentages of women among the sciences: psychology, 9.8; zoology, 7.5; chemistry, 2.1; physics and geology, 1.3. For comparable statistics in 1921 and 1938, based on the third and sixth editions of *AMS,* see Rossiter (1982:136), who gives 20.4 percent and 21.7 percent as the proportion of women in psychology for these years. Of the fifteen sciences she lists, only nutrition exceeded psychology in the proportion of women in the field.

Chapter 1. The Quest for Graduate Education: Mary Calkins' Contest with Harvard University

1. For a fascinating account of Durant and the early all-women professoriate at Wellesley College, see Palmieri (1981).

2. In fact, in the 1870s and 1880s, when graduate study was just getting

started in the United States, even institutions such as John Hopkins and Harvard could not always find men with the requisite training for their faculties. On more than one occasion, they resorted to hiring promising individuals and sending them off to study a particular field for two or three years (see Hawkins 1960 and 1972).

3. "Physiological psychology" was used as a synonym for the new psychology in the late nineteenth century. "Physiological" as a modifier for "psychology" indicated that this approach to psychology was the newer experimental one rather than the older speculative and philosophical approach.

4. See Sokal (1981:1–11) for an excellent general account of the influx of American students into German universities in the nineteenth century.

5. See Sokal (1980, 1981) for the experience of men studying with Wundt at Leipzig.

6. The enrollment figures are taken from surveys done by the United States Office of Education; the statistics are not broken down by sex prior to 1890 (see John 1935). The best general account of the development of the university in the United States is Veysey (1965). See also Hawkins' work on Johns Hopkins (1960) and Harvard (1972).

7. There are several historical accounts of the Harvard Annex; see especially Schwager (1982) and Buck (1962). For a contemporary view from the perspective of a Harvard professor, see Wendell (1899).

8. Both James, a professor of psychology, and Royce, a philosopher, were members of the Philosophy Department because in the late nineteenth century, psychological laboratories and instruction in the new psychology typically were subsumed under philosophy. It was not until the twentieth century that psychology began breaking away from philosophy to become a separate, autonomous department in colleges and universities, a process that took a long time to complete. Some psychology departments, Harvard's for example, were established as separate entities as late as the 1930s.

9. Herrnstein and Boring (1966), writing on the history of the experimental approach to the study of learning, note that it emerged in the last two decades of the nineteenth century. In a reference to Calkins' research on memory, they observe "she was one of the first in this new field, and she created an experimental technique that is now called the method of paired associates, which has survived to the present time" (530).

10. At the April 10, 1902, meeting of the Radcliffe Academic Board, four women were recommended for the Ph.D. (RABM). In addition to Calkins, they were Lucy Allen Paton and Kate Oelzner Peterson, both of whom did their work in philology, and Ethel Dench Puffer (see chapter 3), who was another student of Münsterberg's in the Philosophy Department. Paton and Puffer accepted the Radcliffe Ph.D. offer; Calkins and Peterson declined.

11. Radcliffe archivist Jane S. Knowles has brought to our attention that beginning in 1892 there were combined graduate-undergraduate courses

offered at the Harvard Annex. However, in 1894 when Radcliffe replaced the Annex and all Harvard graduate courses were opened to Radcliffe students, the number of these graduate-undergraduate courses offered at Radcliffe plummeted.

12. Another attempt to secure the Harvard Ph.D. for Calkins was made in 1927, the year after Johns Hopkins had belatedly awarded the doctorate, which she had earned in 1882, to Christine Ladd-Franklin (see chapter 5). A group of psychologists and philosophers, all Harvard degree holders, sent a petition to President Abbott Lowell requesting that Harvard follow the precedent of Johns Hopkins by awarding Calkins the Ph.D. she had earned in the 1890s. The Harvard Corporation considered and refused this request, saying they could see no adequate reason for granting her the degree (Furumoto 1979, 1980).

13. No scholarly historical treatment exists of the graduate education of women at Harvard from the 1890s to the 1960s. Accounts published under the auspices of Radcliffe College (see for example Faculty-Trustee Committee 1956 and Howells 1978) do not discuss where women were actually receiving their instruction. These works do not mention that to be a Radcliffe student was to be a woman student in a Harvard graduate program.

14. Additional biographical information on Mary Calkins is provided in the following accounts: M. Calkins (1930), R. Calkins (1931), and Furumoto (1979, 1980).

2. The Family Claim: Ties That Bound Milicent Shinn

1. There is very little published biographical material on Shinn other than the entry by Burnham in *Notable American Women* (1971b). We would like to acknowledge John Burnham's helpfulness in giving us the research notes that he collected while preparing the Shinn biography. One other account of her life and contributions can be found in her obituary in the *New York Times* on August 15, 1940.

2. Many women who had already completed college courses elsewhere were attracted to the Annex by the opportunity to pursue advanced study with Harvard professors (see Schwager 1982: ch. 5). For example, Mary Calkins (see our chapter 1), who had already completed her A.B. at Smith and wanted advanced work in psychology, considered taking courses in the Annex.

3. The "Intolerable Choice": Ethel Puffer's Struggle with the Marriage versus Career Dilemma

1. For a discussion of faculty life at several women's colleges in the nineteenth and early twentieth centuries, see Horowitz (1984). Palmieri (1983) provides a detailed description of faculty relationships at Wellesley College.

2. See Hayden (1981) and Mohraz (n.d.) for fuller accounts of the circumstances surrounding the demise of the institute.

4. *Meritocracy in Science: Margaret Floy Washburn's Use of the Myth*

1. Cole (1979) provided a comprehensive examination of meritocracy in science as applied to women, concluding that sex-based discrimination against women scientists is negligible. In a later publication, however, he acknowledged that bias still exists in certain areas (Cole 1981). Cole's work has been thoughtfully discussed by Bernard (1982).

2. This chapter incorporates interviews with students and colleagues of "Miss Washburn" who have generously shared their impressions and remembrances of her: Lucy Day Boring, Annette Gillette, Mary Cover Jones, Louise Marshall, Lois Barclay Murphy, and Jean Rowley.

3. Information on her family is found in Washburn's autobiography (1932), her notes for Michael Floy's diary (Brooks 1941), and a form she filed when elected to the National Academy of Sciences in 1932.

4. Edith Wharton's novels, especially *Age of Innocence,* are a good source for portrayals of New York society in the last decades of the nineteenth century.

5. The required senior course, usually taught by the college president (who was often a clergyman) and titled "moral philosophy," filled an important function in providing ethical training for college graduates, fitting them for the world in which they were expected to take a leadership role. At least that was the intention in instructing young men. The women's colleges, endeavoring to provide equal education, also required the course.

6. At that time it was still common for women faculty members to live on campus with the students. Their responsibilities extended beyond classroom instruction, for they were expected to assist in the social and moral development of students as well (Horowitz 1984).

7. Rossiter (1982:71-72) discusses the plight of women who served as deans, noting that "though the deans were usually required to have doctorates, they were only barely tolerated on the institutions' often nearly all-male faculties."

8. For additional discussions of Washburn's life and career see Boring (1971), Dallenbach (1940), Goodman (1980a), Pillsbury (1940), and Woodworth (1949).

9. Florence Sabin, an anatomist holding the M.D. from Johns Hopkins, was the first woman elected to the National Academy of Sciences.

10. A glaring example of the attitude that prevailed for many years is given in a letter written by E. G. Boring, who was then at Clark University but on his way to an appointment at Harvard. In responding to a colleague's search for new faculty, he discussed three men as possibilities, describing

their qualifications at some length, and then concluded: "I will keep you in mind, and if I think of anyone else make suggestions. You do not know of anyone who wants a good girl as instructor next year, do you? Miss Marjory Bates takes her degree with me in June and is first-class except for the limitation of her sex" (to Walter B. Pillsbury, May 8, 1922, WBPP).

11. Washburn "never attempted to develop graduate study at Vassar, since she deprecated such study for women at any but coeducational universities" (Woodworth 1949:278). Though her career would have been enhanced by directing a graduate program and sending out disciples as "her" students, she "felt deeply that women's education should be the same as that for men" (Boring 1971:548). It may be that she realized it would be more beneficial for her women students to seek graduate degrees at a well-known, coeducational institution. If so, she was correctly anticipating what came to be commonplace knowledge: that "it is to the student's advantage to attend one of the major universities. . . . Regardless of the candidate's own merit, some of the prestige of the institution accrues to him [sic] merely by virtue of his attendance, since he profits by the 'halo effect.' " (B. Berelson, cited in Bernard 1964:86). Most of Washburn's students who went on to doctoral study did so at Columbia.

12. See the report of the Association of American Colleges' Project on Redefining the Meaning and Purpose of Baccalaureate Degrees (Integrity in the College Curriculum 1985) for an appraisal of what the shift of faculty loyalty from institution to discipline has meant for higher education. Bernard (1964: ch. 6) discusses women's preference for teaching as a vocation.

13. Cole (1979: ch. 6) sketches those values and how they created "marginal women" around the turn of the century.

14. Washburn was here using the analogy between racial and sexual discrimination that was debated so heatedly in the 1960s and 1970s. For a lucid discussion of that issue, see Chafe (1977: chs. 3 and 4). Cadwallader (1984:33–39) provides details of Turner's career.

15. The "triple penalty" was described by Zuckerman and Cole (1975).

5. "A Little Hard on Ladies": Christine Ladd-Franklin's Challenge to Collegial Exclusion

1. We would like to acknowledge the help of Nancy R. Werth, whose unpublished paper on Ladd-Franklin's letters to the editor of the *Nation* and the *New York Times* drew our attention to these contributions, many of which were unsigned.

2. By 1904 women constituted 5.5 percent of the members elected to the APA and they were active participants at the annual meetings. This may well be another reason why the APA did not meet Titchener's needs.

3. We are grateful to Ben Harris for calling our attention to Christine

Ladd-Franklin's early diaries in the Vassar College Archives and for sharing with us his copies and transcriptions of their contents.

4. June Etta Downey (1875–1932) was clearly an early eminent woman psychologist. In this book she is not considered part of the first generation because she did not appear in *American Men of Science* until the second (1910) edition and she had not become a member of APA by 1906. For biographical accounts of Downey see *Notable American Women* (1971) and Van Horn and Furumoto (1985).

5. We appreciate the helpful comments and suggestions of Alfred H. Fuchs on an earlier version of this chapter. Sharing with us his own experience in academia, he underscored the importance for career building of having access to the "old-boy network," and he called our attention to the Larson and Sullivan (1965) article.

6. The Experimentalists were not the last group of psychologists to engage in exclusionary practices against women. In the mid-1930s several young experimental psychologists in the East were becoming increasingly dissatisfied with the lack of a proper forum for their research. Senior men in the discipline dominated both the APA and the Society of Experimental Psychologists. In 1936 these young psychologists organized a group that was to become known as the Psychological Round Table, which Benjamin argues played a major role as a communication network "in what could be called the middle period of American psychology" (1977:549). Attendance at the meetings was by invitation only, and according to Benjamin "while there was no formal policy that prevented women from receiving invitations, women were nevertheless not invited" (544).

6. Origins, Education, and Life-Styles

1. The women's birthdates range from 1847 to 1883, a 36-year span. All but seven (71 percent) were born in the 1860s and 1870s, with half being born before 1869, half after.

2. For a brief discussion of the opening of graduate instruction to women, see Woody (1929, 2:333–40). Solomon (1985:133–38) provides a more recent treatment. Rossiter (1982) has amply documented the dismal situation for women in the established sciences of the late nineteenth century; see especially her chapter 4.

3. The concern about professionalism that psychologists displayed reflected a widespread social phenomenon in America in the latter part of the nineteenth century, ably treated by Bledstein (1976). Rosenberg (1982) discusses some of the men psychologists who encouraged women students. Several of these were married to highly educated women and enthusiastically supported academically ambitious women. The less hospitable situation for women in other sciences is described by Rossiter (1982).

4. Shinn lived all her life in California; Allen was born in Texas. Hamlin's father was a missionary-educator in Turkey where she lived for several years before the family returned to New England. M. K. Smith, born in Nova Scotia and educated in part in Europe, nevertheless attended a normal school in New York. The others were natives of New England (Massachusetts, 3; Connecticut, 2; Maine, 1), Pennsylvania (3), New York (3 including 2 in New York City), and the Midwest (Iowa, 2; Ohio, 2; Wisconsin, 2; Illinois, 1; Minnesota, 1).

5. There were no Catholics or Jews in this group. Naomi Norsworthy, whom Rossiter (1982:115) suggests was a Jew, was in fact the daughter of parents born in England and, following her mother and her paternal grandmother, held throughout her life to a rigid faith in the tenets of the "Plymouth Brethren," a religious group similar in beliefs to the Quakers (Higgins 1918:18–29).

6. M. K. Smith graduated with a "classical diploma" from Oswego State Normal School (New York) in 1883. Moore earned a "certificate of proficiency" in biology from University of Pennsylvania in 1890 after two years' study, and Prichard was a graduate of the Philadelphia Normal School for Girls (1867). Only in 1894 did it become possible for a woman in Philadelphia to enroll for a science baccalaureate degree (in biology at the University of Pennsylvania).

7. Women's colleges where these women studied were: Vassar, 4; Smith, 3; Wellesley, 3; Radcliffe; and Wilson. State universities included Ohio, Michigan, Iowa, Nebraska, California, and Washington. Private coeducational institutions were: Chicago, 2; Columbia Teachers College; and Hamline.

8. Institutions granting women Ph.D.s in psychology were: Cornell, 5; Chicago, 4; Radcliffe (for study at Harvard), 3; Pennsylvania, 2; Columbia Teachers College; Yale; Iowa; California; and Zürich. In 1894 *A Handbook for Graduate Students,* produced by the Harvard Graduate Club, listed the eleven best universities in the country. Only four of these both admitted women and had doctoral programs in psychology in the 1890s—Chicago, Cornell, Yale, and Pennsylvania.

9. Sixty percent of the men who were APA members in 1907 held Ph.D.s from Harvard, Columbia, Yale, Clark, Cornell, Leipzig, Hopkins, and Chicago, in descending order of representation. These universities were obviously the favored sites for advanced study in psychology.

10. The fact that several women continued their study through the master's level before leaving college suggests an ambivalence about future plans. The master's degree represented at most an extended nonspecific liberal arts program (John 1935), and continued education after college may have been only a way of deferring inevitable and difficult choices about where to live, what to do, and whether to marry.

11. Lagemann (1979) has published the educational biographies of five

progressive reformers, who differed from the psychologists especially in that they did not have the strong academic orientation of the women who pursued doctoral education.

12. Horowitz (1984) has described the particular characteristics of several different institutions and includes an insightful chapter on faculty life.

7. Careers and Contributions

1. Two married immediately—Bagley and Ladd-Franklin; Moore had married a few years earlier; and Shinn returned to her family and subsequently did not hold a paid position.

2. A report in 1904 listed three types of psychological laboratories, classified according to the value of their apparatus. Fourteen institutions had equipment valued from $3,000 to $12,000. All the others had less than $2,000 worth of equipment, placing them in the lowest category, and this group included Bryn Mawr, Mt. Holyoke, Randolph Macon, Vassar, and Wellesley—the only women's colleges listed as having laboratories (Miner 1904).

3. See Morawski (1982) and Napoli (1981) for discussions of early psychologists' proposals for the role of psychology in societal improvement.

4. In the ninth (1956) and tenth (1962) editions of *AMS,* Allen's listing is followed by that of her son, W. W. Charters, Jr.

5. See Adams (1920:54–60). Here she gave her own definition of the professional worker: "the liberally educated person in action, bringing all his resources of training and experience and personality to bear upon a specific problem of production or construction" (56).

6. Visher (1939) discusses the starred psychologists. During the years 1903 to 1943, the fields having the highest proportion of women distinguished by stars were psychology, zoology, and anthropology, although by 1943 only two women psychologists had been added to the six women of the first generation who received stars.

7. Miner (1904:301) lists courses in "physiological psychology and abnormal psychology; genetic psychology and child study; historical, analytical, and systematic psychology; the psychology of the emotions and will, the psychology of logic, of esthetics, of ethics and of religion; the application of statistical methods to psychology; experimental phonetics." Pillsbury (1917) adds child study and use of statistics in educational applications, mental pathology, tests of intelligence, animal psychology, general theory development, and practical applications in business settings as areas that opened up in the following years. Note the addition of applied subjects during this period.

8. In 1917 Cattell reported that of the 307 members in the APA, 272 were engaged in teaching, a "larger percentage than in any other science

except mathematics." Most of the others had also taught, but of these, 11 were engaged in work unrelated to psychology. Cattell speculated that this was the case for married women (having taught but then moved to "unrelated work"), as there were 9 women among the 11 (1917:278). Here Cattell was tacitly acknowledging that a married woman was expected to leave teaching, which also meant—for her—leaving the field.

9. The index is a fair indicator of one's work in psychology but cannot be accepted as providing full bibliographies because many of these psychologists published in the literature of cognate fields such as education and philosophy.

10. Completion of doctoral study in psychology clearly qualified the women for APA membership, though it was not an absolute requirement; in 1907, 17 percent of APA members did not have Ph.D.s. The women doctorates were elected apparently without any objections from the men, and several who lacked the Ph.D. were also elected. In our group of 25, only 4 did not become members of APA. As none of these identified themselves as psychologists, it is not surprising that they did not join the APA. Rather it is curious that they were included in *AMS*. Presumably 3 of the 4 were listed because they had undertaken doctoral study and published their psychology-related research.

11. A research report by Calkins, "Statistics of Dreams," presented by E. C. Sanford, was among the 12 papers comprising the program at the first annual meeting in 1892, and Franklin had published in the *American Journal of Psychology*.

12. We are indebted to Michael M. Sokal for calling our attention to the Cattell material that appears in an undated notebook of his draft letters.

13. At the 80th APA meeting in 1972, Anne Anastasi served as president, followed the next year by Leona E. Tyler.

8. To the Present

1. Camfield (1973) discusses the efforts of early psychologists to establish psychology as a discipline in academia and to gain recognition for psychology as a science around the turn of the century. He argues that in the period between 1904 and 1917 psychologists shifted their focus to elevating the stature of the field.

2. Nieva and Gutek (1980) review research that documents the widespread devaluation of work done by or attributed to women. One of their conclusions is that studies imply "that bias has maximally detrimental effects on women who are competent" (273). As one example, a later report showed that "an article written by a male was evaluated more favorably than if the author was not male" (Paludi and Bauer 1983:387).

3. Benjamin (1985) suggests yet another reason for the low status of

applied psychology: that in the 1930s psychology was called to task for having promised more than it could deliver when the problems of the Depression seemed to defy remedy.

4. Chafe (1972) discusses the narrowing of vision on women's issues that occurred in the early twentieth century and the disillusionment of the early proponents of equality when their hard-won gains were eroded. In chapter 3, "Women in Professions," he specifically addresses circumstances operating in academic life.

5. A rich source of information about how these women proceeded is available in a set of collected autobiographies of accomplished women psychologists born between 1897 and 1922 (O'Connell and Russo 1983).

6. Over the years the purpose of the NCWP changed, as did its name. Its present descendant is the International Council of Psychologists, which includes both men and women as members and seeks to foster cross-cultural understanding and cooperation in addressing human problems.

7. Accomplishments of the CWP since its inception in 1973 are summarized in a recent report (Committee on Women in Psychology 1984).

8. Walsh (1985) discusses some of the developments taking place since the 1940s.

9. See Stocking (1965) for a discussion of the relative merits of "presentism" (studying the past for the sake of the present) and "historicism" (understanding the past for the sake of the past) in doing historical work in the behavioral sciences.

10. Examples of the obliteration phenomenon include failure to recognize Mary Calkins for developing the paired-associates technique (a method for investigating memory) and Margaret Washburn for describing and naming the "goal gradient" concept used by behaviorists.

References

Manuscript Collections

Note: Items from archival sources are identified in the text by the relevant collections according to the code given below. Collections searched for materials that added to our understanding but are not cited in the text include several located at the Archives of the History of American Psychology, Library of Congress, University of Iowa, and Wells College.

CEGP   Charles Edward Garman Papers. Amherst College Archives, Amherst, Mass.

CFP   Calkins Family Papers. Privately held by family.

CLF&FFP   Christine Ladd-Franklin and Fabian Franklin Papers. Rare Book and Manuscript Library, Columbia University, New York City.

CLFP   Christine Ladd-Franklin Papers. Special Collections, Vassar College Library, Poughkeepsie, N.Y.

CR   Corporation Records. Harvard University Archives, Cambridge, Mass.

CWEPP   Charles W. Eliot Presidential Papers. Harvard University Archives, Cambridge, Mass.

DCGP   Daniel Coit Gilman Papers. Special Collections, Milton S. Eisenhower Library, The Johns Hopkins University, Baltimore, Md.

EBTP   Edward Bradford Titchener Papers. Cornell University Archives, Ithaca, N.Y.

ECMP   Ernest Carroll Moore Papers. Special Collections, University Research Library, University of California at Los Angeles, Calif.

EPP   Ethel Puffer Papers. Faculty Papers, Smith College Archives, Northhampton, Mass.

FRDP   Frances Rousmaniere Dewing Papers. Schlesinger Library, Radcliffe College, Cambridge, Mass.

GHHP   George Holmes Howison Papers. Bancroft Library, University of California, Berkeley, Calif.

HMP   Hugo Münsterberg Papers. Boston Public Library, Boston, Mass.

HNGP   H. N. Gardiner Papers. Smith College Archives, Northampton, Mass.

KMcHPC   Keith-McHenry-Pond Collection. Bancroft Library, University of California, Berkeley, Calif.

LOA   Mary Lea Shane Archives of the Lick Observatory. University Library, University of California, Santa Cruz, Calif.

M-HP   Morgan-Howes Papers. Schlesinger Library, Radcliffe College, Cambridge, Mass.

MWCP   Mary Whiton Calkins Papers. Wellesley College Archives, Wellesley, Mass.

PAHP   Phoebe Apperson Hearst Papers. Bancroft Library, University of California, Berkeley, Calif.

RABM   Radcliffe Academic Board Minutes. Radcliffe College Archives, Cambridge, Mass.

RCA   Radcliffe College Archives. Cambridge, Mass.

RMYP   Robert M. Yerkes Papers. Yale University Library, New Haven, Conn.

WBPP   Walter B. Pillsbury Papers. Michigan Historical Collections, Bentley Historical Library, University of Michigan, Ann Arbor, Mich.

WCA   Records of the Class of 1898. Wellesley College Archives, Wellesley, Mass.

Bibliography

Note: Due to burgeoning scholarship in both women's history and history of psychology during the past decade, the literature base for topics considered in this book is vast. We have included here only those references cited in the text and our chapter notes.

Adams, Elizabeth Kemper. 1920. "Some New Professional Standards for College Women." *Educational Record* 1:54–60.
Adams, Elizabeth Kemper. 1921. *Women Professional Workers: A Study Made for the Women's Educational and Industrial Union.* New York: Macmillan.
Adams, Grace. 1931. "Titchener at Cornell." *American Mercury* 24:440–46.
Addams, Jane. 1902. *Democracy and Social Ethics.* Reprint, with introduction by Anne Firor Scott. Cambridge: Harvard University Press, Belknap Press, 1964.
Anderson, John. 1933. "The Methods of Child Psychology." In Carl Murchison, ed., *A Handbook of Child Psychology,* pp.3–28. Worcester, Mass.: Clark University Press.
Antler, Joyce. 1977. "The Educated Woman and Professionalization: The Struggle for a New Feminine Identity, 1890–1920." Ph.D. diss., State University of New York at Stony Brook.
Antler, Joyce. 1980. "After College, What?: New Graduates and the Family Claim." *American Quarterly* 32:409–34.
Barus, Annie Howse. 1895. Report of the Committee on the Study of Child Development, of the Association of Collegiate Alumnae. In *National Educational Association: Journal of Proceedings and Addresses of the Year 1894,* pp. 996–99. New York: National Education Association.
Benjamin, Ludy T., Jr. 1977. "The Psychological Round Table: Revolution of 1936." *American Psychologist* 32:542–49.
Benjamin, Ludy T., Jr. 1985. "The Selling of Psychology in America: 1885–1985." Paper read at annual meeting of the Rocky Mountain Psychological Association, Tucson, Ariz.
Berkin, Carol Ruth and Mary Beth Norton, eds. 1979. *Women of America: A History.* Boston: Houghton Mifflin.
Bernard, Jessie. 1964. *Academic Women.* Reprint. New York: New American Library, Meridian Books, 1974.
Bernard, Jessie. 1983. "Benchmark for the '80s." In Mary L. Spencer, Monika Kehoe, and Karen Speece, eds., *Handbook for Women Scholars: Strategies for Success,* pp. 69–79. San Francisco: Center for Women Scholars.
Bjork, Daniel W. 1983. *The Compromised Scientist: William James in the Development of American Psychology.* New York: Columbia University Press.
Bledstein, Burton J. 1976. *The Culture of Professionalism: The Middle Class and the Development of Higher Education in America.* New York: Norton.

Boring, Edwin G. 1920. "Statistics of the American Psychological Association in 1920." *Psychological Bulletin* 17:271–78.

Boring, Edwin G. 1938. "The Society of Experimental Psychologists." *American Journal of Psychology* 51:410–21.

Boring, Edwin G. 1967. "Titchener's Experimentalists." *Journal of the History of the Behavioral Sciences* 3:315–25.

Boring, Edwin G. 1971. "Margaret Floy Washburn." In Edward T. James, Janet Wilson James, and Paul S. Boyer, eds., *Notable American Women, 1607–1950,* 3:546–48. Cambridge: Harvard University Press, Belknap Press.

Bradbury, Dorothy E. 1937. "The Contribution of the Child Study Movement to Child Psychology." *Psychological Bulletin* 34:21–38.

Brooks, Richard Albert Edward, ed. 1941. *The Diary of Michael Floy, Jr., Bowery Village, 1833–1837.* New Haven: Yale University Press.

Brumberg, Joan Jacobs and Nancy Tomes. 1982. "Women in the Professions: A Research Agenda for American Historians." *Reviews in American History* 10:275–96.

Bryan, Alice I. and Edwin G. Boring. 1947. "Women in American Psychology: Factors Affecting Their Professional Careers." *American Psychologist* 2:3–20.

Buchner, Edward Franklin. 1909. "Psychological Progress in 1908." *Psychological Bulletin* 6:1–13.

Buck, Paul. 1962. "Harvard Attitudes toward Radcliffe in the Early Years." In *Proceedings of the Massachusetts Historical Society,* pp. 33–50. Boston.

Burnham, John Chynoweth. 1971a. "Lillien Jane Martin." In Edward T. James, Janet Wilson James, and Paul S. Boyer, eds., *Notable American Women, 1607–1950,* 2:504–5. Cambridge: Harvard University Press, Belknap Press.

Burnham, John Chynoweth. 1971b. "Milicent Washburn Shinn." In Edward T. James, Janet Wilson James, and Paul S. Boyer, eds., *Notable American Women, 1607–1950,* 3:285–86. Cambridge: Harvard University Press, Belknap Press.

Cadwallader, Thomas C. 1984. "Neglected Aspects of the Evolution of American Comparative and Animal Psychology." In Gary Greenberg and Ethel Tobach, eds., *Behavioral Evolution and Integrative Levels,* pp. 15–48. Hillsdale, N.J.: Lawrence Erlbaum.

Cairns, Robert B. 1983. "The Emergence of Developmental Psychology." In Paul H. Mussen, ed., *Handbook of Child Psychology,* 4th ed. Vol. 1: William Kessen, ed., *History, Theory, and Methods,* pp. 41–102. New York: Wiley.

Calkins, Mary Whiton. 1896. "Association: An Essay Analytic and Experimental." *Psychological Monographs* 1:1–56.

Calkins, Mary Whiton. 1930. "Mary Whiton Calkins." In Carl Murchison, ed., *A History of Psychology in Autobiography,* 1:31–62. Worchester, Mass.: Clark University Press.

Calkins, Raymond. 1931. "Mary Whiton Calkins." In *In Memoriam: Mary Whiton Calkins 1863–1930,* pp. 1–19. Boston: Merrymount Press.

Camfield, Thomas M. 1973. "The Professionalization of American Psychology, 1870–1917." *Journal of the History of the Behavioral Sciences* 9:66–75.

Cattell, James McKeen, ed. 1906. *American Men of Science: A Biographical Directory.* New York: Science Press.

Cattell, James McKeen. 1917. "Our Psychological Association and Research." *Science* 45:275–84.

Cattell, James McKeen and Jaques Cattell, eds. 1933. *American Men of Science,* 5th ed. New York: Science Press.

Caullery, Maurice. 1922. *Universities and Scientific Life in the United States.* Trans. James Haughton Woods and Emmet Russell. Cambridge: Harvard University Press.

Chafe, William H. 1972. *The American Woman: Her Changing Social, Economic, and Political Roles, 1920–1970.* New York: Oxford University Press.

Chafe, William H. 1977. *Women and Equality: Changing Patterns in American Culture.* New York: Oxford University Press.

Chrisman, Oscar. 1900. Review of Milicent Washburn Shinn, *Notes on the Development of a Child,* pts. 3–4. *Educational Review* 20:192–94.

Cole, Jonathan R. 1979. *Fair Science: Women in the Scientific Community.* New York: Free Press.

Cole, Jonathan R. 1981. "Women in Science." *American Scientist* 69:385–91.

Committee on Women in Psychology. 1984. *Women in the American Psychological Association.* Washington: American Psychological Association.

Conable, Charlotte Williams. 1977. *Women at Cornell: The Myth of Equal Education.* Ithaca, N.Y.: Cornell University Press.

Cott, Nancy F. 1977. *The Bonds of Womanhood: Woman's Sphere in New England, 1780–1835.* New Haven: Yale University Press.

Cott, Nancy F. and Elizabeth H. Pleck, eds. 1979. *A Heritage of Her Own: Toward a New Social History of American Women.* New York: Simon and Schuster.

Dallenbach, Karl M. 1940. "Margaret Floy Washburn." *Journal of Psychology* 53:1–5.

Darley, John M., Sam Glucksberg, and Ronald A. Kinchla. 1981. *Psychology.* 3d ed. Englewood Cliffs, N.J.: Prentice-Hall.

deFord, Miriam Allen. 1948. *Psychologist Unretired: The Life Pattern of Lillien J. Martin.* Stanford: Stanford University Press.

Eberts, Cindelyn Gray and Philip Howard Gray. 1982. "Evaluating the Historical Treatment of Female Psychologists of Distinction Using Citation Analysis and Textbook Coverage." *Bulletin of the Psychonomic Society* 20:7–10.

Faculty-Trustee Committee. 1956. *Graduate Education for Women: The Radcliffe Ph.D.* Cambridge: Harvard University Press.

Faderman, Lillian. 1981. *Surpassing the Love of Men: Romantic Friendship and Love between Women from the Renaissance to the Present.* New York: William Morrow.

Fernberger, Samuel W. 1928. "Statistical Analyses of the Members and Associates of the American Psychological Association, Inc. in 1928." *Psychological Review* 35:447–65.

Fernberger, Samuel W. 1932. "The American Psychological Association, a Historical Summary, 1892–1930." *Psychological Bulletin* 29:1–89.

Fernberger, Samuel W. 1939. "Academic Psychology as a Career for Women." *Psychological Bulletin* 36:390–94.

Finison, Lorenz J. and Laurel Furumoto. 1980. "Status of Women in American Psychology, 1890–1940, or on How to Win the Battles yet Lose the War." Paper read at annual meeting of the Cheiron Society, New Brunswick, Me.

Fisher, S. Carolyn, J. A. Gengerelli, F. Nowell Jones, and May V. Seagoe. 1965. "Kate Gordon Moore." In *University of California In Memoriam.* Berkeley: University of California Press.

Footner, Hulbert. 1937. *New York, City of Cities.* Philadelphia: Lippincott.

Frith, Gladys D. 1939. "Psychology as a Profession." *Women's Work and Education* 10(October): 1–3.

Furumoto, Laurel. 1979. "Mary Whiton Calkins (1863–1930): Fourteenth President of the American Psychological Association." *Journal of the History of the Behavioral Sciences* 15:346–56.

Furumoto, Laurel. 1980. "Mary Whiton Calkins (1863–1930)." *Psychology of Women Quarterly* 5:55–68.

Furumoto, Laurel. 1984. Review of Agnes N. O'Connell and Nancy F. Russo, eds., *Models of Achievement: Reflections of Eminent Women in Psychology.* *Sex Roles* 11:558–62.

Furumoto, Laurel. 1985. "Placing Women in the History of Psychology Course." *Teaching of Psychology* 12:203–6.

Furumoto, Laurel and Elizabeth Scarborough. 1986. "Placing Women in the History of Psychology: The First American Women Psychologists." *American Psychologist* 41:35–42.

Gamble, Eleanor A. McC. 1929. "The Psychology of the Modern Girl." Paper read at meeting of the Association of Principals of Secondary Schools, Cleveland, Ohio.

[Garfield, Eugene.] 1975. "The 'Obliteration Phenomenon' in Science—and the Advantage of Being Obliterated!" Reprinted in *Essays of an Information Scientist,* 2:396–98. Philadelphia: ISI Press, 1977.

Gilman, Charlotte Perkins. 1906. "The Passing of Matrimony." *Harper's Bazar* 40:495–98.

Goodman, Elizabeth S[carborough]. 1980a. "Margaret F. Washburn (1871–1939): First Woman Ph.D. in Psychology." *Psychology of Women Quarterly* 5:69–80.

Goodman, Elizabeth S[carborough]. 1980b. "Student Collaborators of Margaret Floy Washburn." Paper read at annual meeting of the Eastern Psychological Association, Hartford, Conn.

Goodman, Elizabeth S[carborough]. 1980c. "Women in APA: The First Thirty Years (1892–1921)." Paper read at annual meeting of the American Psychological Association, Montreal, Que.

Goodman, Elizabeth S[carborough]. 1983. "History's Choices." Review of J. F. Brennan, *History and Systems of Psychology,* and D. J. Murray, *A History of Western Psychology. Contemporary Psychology* 28:667–69.

Goodwin, C. James. 1985. "On the Origins of Titchener's Experimentalists." *Journal of the History of the Behavioral Sciences* 21:383–89.

Gordon, Kate. 1905. "Wherein Should the Education of a Woman Differ from That of a Man." *School Review* 13:789–94.

Gordon, Kate. 1924. "Group Judgements in the Field of Lifted Weights." *Journal of Experimental Psychology* 7:398–400.

Gordon, Sarah H. 1975. "Smith College Students: The First Ten Classes, 1879–1888." *History of Education Quarterly* 15:147–67.

Hale, Matthew, Jr. 1980. *Human Science and Social Order: Hugo Münsterberg and the Origins of Applied Psychology.* Philadelphia: Temple University Press.

[Hall, G. Stanley.] 1887. "Editorial Note." *American Journal of Psychology* 1:3–4.

Hall, G. Stanley. 1904. *Adolescence,* vol. 2. New York: Appleton.

Hall, G. Stanley. 1914. Obituary. *Pedagogical Seminary* 21:160.

Hall, G. Stanley and Theodate L. Smith. 1903. "Marriage and Fecundity of College Men and Women." *Pedagogical Seminary* 10:273–314.

Hawkins, Hugh. 1960. *Pioneer: A History of the Johns Hopkins University, 1874–1889.* Ithaca, N.Y.: Cornell University Press.

Hawkins, Hugh. 1972. *Between Harvard and America: The Educational Leadership of Charles W. Eliot.* New York: Oxford University Press.

Hayden, Dolores. 1981. *The Grand Domestic Revolution: A History of Feminist Designs for American Homes, Neighborhoods, and Cities.* Cambridge: MIT Press.

Heidbreder, Edna. 1972. "Mary Whiton Calkins: A Discussion." *Journal of the History of the Behavioral Sciences* 8:56–68.

Helmer, Bessie Bradwell. N.d. Association of Collegiate Alumnae, Report of the Committee on Fellowships.

Herrnstein, Richard J. and Edwin G. Boring, eds. 1966. *A Sourcebook in the History of Psychology.* Cambridge: Harvard University Press.

Higgins, Frances Caldwell. 1918. *The Life of Naomi Norsworthy.* New York: Houghton Mifflin.

Holt, Edwin B. 1915. *The Freudian Wish and Its Place in Ethics.* New York: Henry Holt.

Horowitz, Helen Lefkowitz. 1984. *Alma Mater: Design and Experience in the Women's Colleges from their Nineteenth Century Beginnings to the 1930s.* New York: Knopf.

Howells, Dorothy Elia. 1978. *A Century to Celebrate: Radcliffe College, 1879–1979.* Cambridge: Radcliffe College.

Howes, Ethel Puffer. 1922a. " 'Accepting the Universe.' " *Atlantic Monthly* 129:444–53.

Howes, Ethel Puffer. 1922b. "Continuity for Women." *Atlantic Monthly* 130:731–39.

Howes, Ethel Puffer. 1923. "True and Substantial Happiness." *Woman's Home Companion,* December issue.

Howes, Ethel Puffer. 1929. "The Meaning of Progress in the Woman Movement." *Annals of the American Academy of Political and Social Science* 143:14–20.

Howes, Ethel Puffer. 1937. "The Golden Age." *Radcliffe Quarterly* 21:14–16.

"Integrity in the College Curriculum." 1985. Report of the Association of American College's Project on Redefining the Meaning and Purpose of Baccalaureate Degrees. *Chronicle of Higher Education,* February 13 issue.

James, Henry. 1930. *Charles W. Eliot: President of Harvard University 1869–1909,* vol. 2. Boston: Houghton Mifflin.

Jewett, Louise Rogers and Mary Whiton Calkins, eds. 1910. *The Poems of Sophie Jewett,* 2d ed. New York: Thomas Y. Crowell.

John, Walton C. 1935. *Graduate Study in Universities and Colleges in the United States.* Washington, D.C.: United States Government Printing Office.

Jones, Lewis L. 1978. "Carl Emil Seashore: Dean of the Graduate College of the University of Iowa, 1908 to 1936, Dean *pro tempore,* 1942 to 1946: A Study of His Ideas on Graduate Education." Ph.D. diss., University of Iowa.

Kessen, William, Marshall M. Haith, and Philip H. Salapatek. 1970. "Infancy." In Paul H. Mussen, ed., *Carmichael's Manual of Child Psychology,* 3d ed., 1:287–445. New York: Wiley.

Ladd-Franklin, Christine. 1887. "A Method for the Experimental Determination of the Horopter." *American Journal of Psychology* 1:99–111.

[Ladd-Franklin, Christine.] 1889. "College Life for Women." *The Nation* 49:326–27.

[Ladd-Franklin, Christine.] 1890. "Vassar College." *The Nation* 50:483–84.

[Ladd-Franklin, Christine.] 1891a. Review of Mary Wollstonecraft, *A Vindication of the Rights of Woman,* new edition. *The Nation* 52:163–64.

[Ladd-Franklin, Christine.] 1891b. Review of Ch. Letourneau, *The Evolution of Marriage. The Nation* 53:52–53.

[Ladd-Franklin, Christine.] 1896a. Review of Lina Eckenstein, *Woman Under Monasticism. The Nation* 63:90-91.

[Ladd-Franklin, Christine.] 1896b. Review of Phebe Mitchell Kendall, *Maria Mitchell: Life, Letters, and Journals. The Nation* 63:235–37.

[Ladd-Franklin, Christine.] 1901. Review of Milicent W. Shinn, *The Biography of a Baby. The Nation* 72:142.

Ladd-Franklin, Christine. 1929. *Colour and Colour Theories.* New York: Harcourt, Brace.

Lagemann, Ellen Condliffe. 1979. *A Generation of Women: Education in the Lives of Progressive Reformers.* Cambridge: Harvard University Press.

Larson, Cedric A. and John J. Sullivan. 1965. "Watson's Relation to Titchener." *Journal of the History of the Behavioral Sciences* 1:338–54.

Lerner, Gerda. 1979. *The Majority Finds Its Past: Placing Women in History.* New York: Oxford University Press.

Loewenberg, J. and Roelofs, H. D. 1930. Obituary. *Philosophical Review* 39:323.

MacCracken, Henry Noble. 1950. *The Hickory Limb.* New York: Scribner's.

Macurdy, Grace Harriet. 1940. "Memories of Margaret Floy Washburn." *Vassar Alumnae Magazine* 25:3–4.

Martin, Lillien Jane and Clare deGruchy. 1933. *Sweeping the Cobwebs.* New York: Macmillan.

Mateer, Florence. 1918. *Child Behavior: A Critical and Experimental Study of Young Children by the Method of Conditioned Reflexes.* Boston: Badger.

Miner, B. G. 1904. "The Changing Attitude of American Universities toward Psychology." *Science* 20:299–307.

Mohraz, Judy Jolley. N.d. "Professional Life after Marriage: The Quest of the Institute for the Coordination of Women's Interests." Photocopy.

Morawski, J. G. 1982. "Assessing Psychology's Moral Heritage through our Neglected Utopias." *American Psychologist* 37:1082–95.

Morison, Samuel Eliot. 1965. *The Oxford History of the American People.* New York: Oxford University Press.

Moore, Kate Gordon. 1944. "Eleanor Harris Rowland Wembridge, 1883–1944." *Psychological Review* 51:326–27.

Münsterberg, Hugo. 1901. "The American Woman." *International Monthly* 3:607–33.

Napoli, Donald S. 1981. *Architects of Adjustment: The History of the Psychological Profession in the United States.* Port Washington, N.Y.: Kennikat Press.

Nieva, Veronica F. and Barbara A. Gutek. 1980. "Sex Effects on Evaluation." *Academy of Management Review* 2:267–76.

Norsworthy, Naomi and Mary Theodora Whitley. 1918. *The Psychology of Childhood.* New York: Macmillan.

Norton, Mary Beth. 1979. "The Paradox of 'Women's Sphere.' " In Carol Ruth Berkin and Mary Beth Norton, eds., *Women of America: A History,* pp. 139–49. Boston: Houghton Mifflin.

O'Connell, Agnes N. and Nancy F. Russo, eds. 1983. *Models of Achievement: Reflections of Eminent Women in Psychology*. New York: Columbia University Press.

Palmieri, Patricia A. 1981. "In Adamless Eden: A Social Portrait of the Academic Community at Wellesley College 1875–1920." Ed.D. diss., Harvard University.

Palmieri, Patricia A. 1983. "Here was Fellowship: A Social Portrait of Academic Women at Wellesley College, 1895–1920." *History of Education Quarterly* 23:195–214.

Paludi, Michele A. and William D. Bauer. 1983. "Goldberg Revisited: What's in an Author's Name." *Sex Roles* 9:387–90.

Pillsbury, W. B. 1917. "The New Developments in Psychology in the Past Quarter Century." *Philosophical Review* 26:56–69.

Pillsbury, W. B. 1940. "Margaret Floy Washburn (1871–1939)." *Psychological Review* 47:99–109.

"Pioneer Women Students in Germany." 1897. *The Nation* 64:262.

Preyer, Wilhelm. 1882. *Die Seele des Kindes* (The Mind of the Child). Leipzig: Grieben.

Puffer, Ethel D. 1905. *The Psychology of Beauty*. Boston: Houghton Mifflin.

Reskin, Barbara F. 1978. "Sex Differentiation and the Social Organization of Science." *Sociological Inquiry* 48:6–37.

Review of Isabel Maddison, *Handbook of Courses Open to Women in British, Continental, and Canadian Universities*. 1896. *The Nation* 63:411.

Rosenberg, Rosalind. 1982. *Beyond Separate Spheres: Intellectual Roots of Modern Feminism*. New Haven: Yale University Press.

Ross, Dorothy. 1972. *G. Stanley Hall: The Psychologist as Prophet*. Chicago: University of Chicago Press.

Ross, Dorothy. 1980. "The Development of the Social Sciences." In Alexandra Oleson and John Voss, eds., *The Organization of Knowledge in Modern America*, pp. 107–38. Baltimore: Johns Hopkins University Press.

Rossiter, Margaret W. 1982. *Women Scientists in America: Struggles and Strategies to 1940*. Baltimore: Johns Hopkins University Press.

Schwager, Sally. 1982. " 'Harvard Women': A History of the Founding of Radcliffe College." Ed.D. diss., Harvard University.

Seashore, Carl E. 1942. "An Open Letter, Addressed to Women in Graduate Schools." *Journal of Higher Education* 13:236–42.

Shinn, Milicent W. 1883. "Thirty Miles." *The Overland Monthly* 1:596–604.

[Shinn, Milicent W.] 1884. "Etc." *The Overland Monthly* 3:103–6.

Shinn, Milicent W. 1893-1899. *Notes on the Development of a Child*. Issued in 3 parts (4 no.). Berkeley: University of California.

Shinn, Milicent W. 1895a. "The First Two Years of the Child." In *Proceedings of the International Congress of Education, Chicago, 1893*. New York: National Education Association.

Shinn, Milicent W. 1895b. "The Marriage Rate of College Women." *The Century* 50:946–48.

Shinn, Milicent Washburn. 1900. *The Biography of a Baby.* Boston: Houghton Mifflin.

Sokal, Michael M. 1980. "Graduate Study with Wundt: Two Eyewitness Accounts." In Wolfgang G. Bringmann and Ryan J. Tweney, eds., *Wundt Studies: A Centennial Collection,* pp. 210–25. Toronto: C. J. Hogrefe.

Sokal, Michael M., ed. 1981. *An Education in Psychology: James McKeen Cattell's Journal and Letters from Germany and England, 1880–1888.* Cambridge: MIT Press.

Sokal, Michael M. 1984. "The Gestalt Psychologists in Behaviorist America." *American Historical Review* 89:1240–63.

Solomon, Barbara Miller. 1985. *In the Company of Educated Women: A History of Women and Higher Education in America.* New Haven: Yale University Press.

Starr, Kevin. 1973. *Americans and the California Dream, 1850–1915.* New York: Oxford University Press.

Stocking, George W., Jr. 1965. "On the Limits of 'Presentism' and 'Historicism' in the Historiography of the Behavioral Sciences." *Journal of the History of the Behavioral Sciences* 1:211–18.

Thomas, M. Carey. 1908. "Present Tendencies in Women's College and University Education." *Educational Review* 35:64–85.

Thompson, Helen Bradford. 1903. *The Mental Traits of Sex: An Experimental Investigation of the Normal Mind in Men and Women.* Chicago: University of Chicago Press.

Titchener, Edward B. 1910. "The Past Decade in Experimental Psychology." *American Journal of Psychology* 21:404–21.

Van Horn, Christina and Laurel Furumoto. 1985. "June Etta Downey: The Psychologist, the Poet, and the Person." Paper read at annual meeting of the Rocky Mountain Psychological Association, Tucson, Ariz.

Veysey, Laurence R. 1965. *The Emergence of the American University.* Chicago: University of Chicago Press.

Visher, Stephen S. 1939. "Distribution of the Psychologists Starred in the Six Editions of *American Men of Science.*" *American Journal of Psychology* 52:278–92.

Walsh, Mary Roth. 1977. *"Doctors Wanted: No Women Need Apply": Sexual Barriers in the Medical Profession 1935–1975.* New Haven: Yale University Press.

Walsh, Mary Roth. 1985. "Academic Professional Women Organizing for Change: The Struggle in Psychology." *Journal of Social Issues* 41:17–27.

Washburn, Margaret Floy. 1908. *The Animal Mind, a Textbook of Comparative Psychology.* New York: Macmillan.

Washburn, Margaret Floy. 1932. "Some Recollections." In C. Murchison, ed., *A History of Psychology in Autobiography*, 2:333–58. Worcester, Mass.: Clark University Press.

Welter, Barbara. 1966. "The Cult of True Womanhood." *American Quarterly* 18:151–74.

Wendell, Barrett. 1899. "The Relations of Radcliffe College with Harvard." *The Harvard Monthly* 29:1–10.

Woodworth, Robert S. 1930. "Christine Ladd-Franklin." *Science* 71:307.

Woodworth, Robert S. 1949. "Margaret Floy Washburn." In *National Academy of Sciences Biographical Memoirs*, 25:273–95. Washington: National Academy of Sciences.

Woody, Thomas. 1929. *A History of Women's Education in the United States*, vol. 2. New York: Octagon Books, 1966.

Yerkes, Robert M., ed. 1921. *Memoirs of the National Academy of Sciences*, vol. 15. Washington, D.C.: GPO.

Zapoleon, Marguerite W. and Lois Meek Stolz. 1971. "Helen Bradford Thompson Woolley." In Edward T. James, Janet Wilson James, and Paul S. Boyer, eds., *Notable American Women, 1607–1950*, 3:657–60. Cambridge: Harvard University Press, Belknap Press.

Zuckerman, Harriet and J. R. Cole. 1975. "Women in American Science." *Minerva* 13:82–102.

Index

Women in science, 205*n*2; discrimination against, 208*n*1; percentages of in different disciplines, 205*n*4, 205*n*5

Women's colleges: advantages for women faculty at, 150–51, 158; faculty life at, 207*n*1; limitations for faculty at, 103, 158–60

Women's history, field of 8–9

Women's traditional role in nineteenth century, 2–3, 43–44; attitudes of first generation women toward, 146; differences in Germany and U.S., 78; versus professional role, 61, 205*n*2

"Women's work," 162, 168

Woolley, Helen Thompson (Mrs. Paul G.), *see* Thompson, Helen Bradford

Woolley, Paul G., 200

Wundt, Wilhelm, 6, 24, 97, 124, 190

Yale University, 5, 25–26, 116, 188, 198

Yerkes, Robert M., 126

Zürich, University of, 23

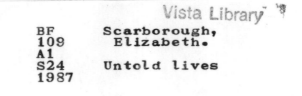